comfort food

comfort food

simple recipes for delicious food every day

RYLAND PETERS & SMALL
LONDON • NEW YORK

Designer Ian Midson

Production Manager Toby Marshall

Art Director Leslie Harrington

Editorial Director Julia Charles

Indexer Hilary Bird

First published in 2013
by Ryland Peters & Small
20–21 Jockey's Fields
London WC1R 4BW
and
519 Broadway, 5th Floor
New York NY 10012

www.rylandpeters.com

Text © Nadia Arumugam, Jordan Bourke,
Maxine Clark, Ross Dobson, Tonia
George, Brian Glover, Jennifer Joyce,
Dan May, Annie Rigg, Sonia Stevenson,
Sunil Vijayakar, Laura Washburn and
Ryland Peters & Small 2013

Design and photographs © Ryland
Peters & Small 2013

ISBN: 978-1-84975-450-7

10 9 8 7 6 5 4 3 2 1

A CIP record for this book is available
from the British Library.

US Library of Congress Cataloging-in-
Publication data has been applied for.

Printed and bound in China

notes:

• All spoon measurements are level, unless
otherwise specified.

All herbs used in these recipes are fresh, unless
otherwise specified.

• All fruit and vegetables should be washed
thoroughly before consumption. Unwaxed
citrus fruits should be used whenever possible.

• All eggs are medium UK/large US, unless
otherwise specified. Recipes containing raw or
partially cooked egg should not be served to the
very young, very old, anyone with a compromised
immune system or pregnant women.

contents

home-cooked comforts

In this busy world, it is often hard to find time for the simple things, such as preparing a nice meal for family and friends, but it's always worth spending just a little time in the kitchen to make something warming and comforting. The kitchen can often seem like shelter in a storm and retreating to pots and pans and seeking solace in the stockpot is a good way to take some speed off the pace of modern life. The recipes presented in this book are designed to make it simple to slow down and savour what you eat. Compiled with busy people in mind, many of the dishes can be quickly assembled, then left to simmer, bake or roast, leaving time for other occupations and some can be made in advance so you can cook when you do have time, for enjoyment later on. Most are as suitable for midweek suppers as they are for weekend entertaining.

But spending time in the kitchen is not only good for our frame of mind, it can be good for our bodies. Homemade food can be so much more wholesome, especially when meals are prepared from scratch. So speed and ease of preparation is not the sole consideration; the recipes in this book also offer a way to put good food on the table. Preparing a sustaining snack or a square meal is so much simpler than you think and you can take great comfort in knowing what goes into the food on your plate. Easy, delicious, nutritious; it's hard to do better than that.

These recipes also offer plenty of variety for when you want to liven things up. Alongside traditional comfort food fare – such as mac 'n' cheese, pies and roasts – there are also recipes from India, Morocco, Mexico and Southeast Asia. Not restaurant food, but the kinds of dishes eaten at home, making them straightforward for any cook to prepare regardless of skill, using ingredients that can be found in most supermarkets. Life probably isn't going to slow down anytime soon and cooking is a good antidote and a way to sidestep the chaos. So go on, home cook some comfort today.

Soups are one of the most diverse and endlessly adaptable dishes you can cook and they can be blissfully comforting. Here you'll find hearty classics such as Minestrone and Harrira, as well as new twists to try, such as Parsnip, Chorizo and Chestnut.

soups

roast chicken, garlic & watercress soup

a whole 1.2-kg/2¾-lbs. chicken (small)

3 whole garlic bulbs

a 300-g/10-oz. baking potato

2 tablespoons extra virgin olive oil, plus extra to serve

6 fresh thyme sprigs

900 ml/4 cups chicken stock

150 g/5 oz. watercress

salt and freshly ground black pepper

serves 4

You can either honour this soup by roasting a chicken especially for the occasion or you can buy a ready-roasted chicken. Of course, if you've already roasted a chicken, it's a good way to use up any leftovers. There's nothing more satisfying than two meals from one bird.

Preheat the oven to 200°C (400°F) Gas 6.

Put the chicken in a roasting pan, wrap the garlic bulbs and potato in foil individually and scatter around the edges. Drizzle the olive oil over the chicken, scatter the thyme sprigs over the top and season well. Roast in the preheated oven for 1 hour.

Open the packages of roasted garlic and potato and let cool. At the same time, check that they are really soft inside. If not, return to the oven for a little longer until soft. Pull the chicken meat from the carcass and set aside.

Pour the stock into a large saucepan. Discard the skin from the potato, chop the flesh and add it to the pan. Cut the tops off the garlic bulbs, squeeze out the soft flesh from inside the cloves and add to the soup. Chop up the chicken meat and add that to the soup too. Transfer about a third of the soup to a blender along with the watercress and blend until smooth. Return to the pan and stir until blended. Add more water if you think it's too thick. Season to taste.

Divide the soup between 4 bowls, drizzle with extra olive oil and serve immediately.

split pea & sausage soup

2 tablespoons extra virgin olive oil

1 onion, chopped

1 leek, chopped

2 celery sticks, chopped

a pinch of grated nutmeg

300 g/1½ cups yellow split peas

1.5 litres/6 cups chicken stock

2 dried bay leaves

250 g/8 oz. sausages

salt and freshly ground black pepper

serves 6

This thick wintry mix of tender lentils with chunks of sausage is so filling, it's perfect to get you ready for a long walk, or maybe just a long snooze on the sofa.

Heat the olive oil in a large saucepan and cook the onion, leek and celery gently over low heat for 8–10 minutes. Add the nutmeg and stir to combine. Add the split peas and mix into the vegetables. Add the stock and bay leaves, cover and simmer for 45 minutes or until the peas are tender and beginning to get mushy when pressed with the back of a spoon.

Meanwhile, preheat the grill/broiler to medium–hot. Grill/broil the sausages until cooked, then roughly chop. Add to the soup and cook for a further 10 minutes. Season to taste with salt and freshly ground pepper.

Divide the soup between 6 bowls and serve immediately.

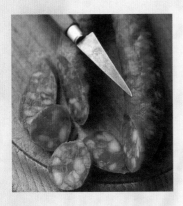

125 g/4 oz. raw chorizo, cubed

1 onion, chopped

3 garlic cloves, sliced

1 celery stick, chopped

1 carrot, chopped

3 parsnips, chopped

¼ teaspoon dried red chilli/hot pepper flakes

1 teaspoon ground cumin

200 g/6½ oz. peeled, cooked chestnuts (fresh or vacuum-packed)

1 litre/4 cups hot chicken stock

salt and freshly ground black pepper

serves 4–6

parsnip, chorizo & chestnut soup

This is a thick and unctuous soup; perfect after building a snowman in the depths of winter. It's very filling so a little goes a long way; serve it as a meal in itself with good crusty bread.

Put the chorizo in a large saucepan and heat gently for 2–3 minutes until the oil seeps out and the chorizo becomes slightly crispy. Lift out the chorizo with a slotted spoon, trying to leave as much oil behind as you can and set aside.

Add the onion, garlic, celery, carrot and parsnips to the pan, stir well, cover and cook gently for 10 minutes, or until softening. Add the dried red chilli/hot pepper flakes and cumin, season with sea salt and freshly ground black pepper and stir to release the aroma. Add the chestnuts and stock, then cover and simmer over low heat for 25–30 minutes until everything is very tender.

Transfer the contents of the pan to a blender and blend until smooth. Reheat the chorizo in a small frying pan.

Divide the soup between 4–6 bowls, scatter with the crispy chorizo and serve immediately.

2 tablespoons extra virgin olive oil

475-g/1-lb. lamb shank

2 onions, sliced

3 celery sticks, chopped

3 garlic cloves, chopped

1 teaspoon ground cinnamon

½ teaspoon saffron threads

½ teaspoon ground ginger

several gratings of nutmeg

1 tablespoon tomato purée/paste

4 tomatoes, chopped

700 ml/2¾ cups stock or water

200-g/7-oz. can chickpeas, drained and rinsed, or dried chickpeas soaked overnight

100 g/½ cup green lentils, rinsed

freshly squeezed juice of 1 lemon

2 tablespoons freshly chopped coriander/cilantro

salt and freshly ground black pepper

serves 4–6

harrira

This is a soup sold all over Morocco. It can be as rustic as you like but this version is defined by the subtle flavour of saffron and accompanying spices. Generally it has a little meat, tomatoes and lots of spices. Serve topped with fresh coriander/cilantro leaves.

Heat the olive oil in a heavy-based casserole dish, then add the lamb and brown evenly. Add the onions, celery, garlic, cinnamon, saffron, ginger and nutmeg and season well. Turn the heat down a little, cover and cook for 10 minutes until soft, stirring occasionally.

Stir in the tomato purée/paste and the tomatoes and cook for a further 2–3 minutes. Add the stock, cover and cook for 1 hour until the lamb is becoming tender.

Add the chickpeas and lentils and cook for a further 40 minutes until they are tender and the lamb can easily be pulled off the bone. Shred the meat from the shank, remove the bone and discard. Add lemon juice to taste and adjust the seasoning, if necessary. Stir in the coriander/cilantro.

Divide the soup between 4–6 bowls and serve immediately.

vietnamese beef pho

1 tablespoon sunflower oil

1 star anise

2 lemongrass stalks, sliced

1 cinnamon stick

1 tablespoon coriander seeds

1 tablespoon black peppercorns

3 cm/1½ inches fresh ginger, sliced

4 garlic cloves, peeled and bruised

1.5 litres/6 cups beef stock

3 sprigs fresh coriander/cilantro

150 g/5 oz. rice noodles

4 tablespoons freshly squeezed lime juice

2 tablespoons fish sauce

200 g/6½ oz. sirloin steak, thinly sliced

100 g/1 cup beansprouts

3 shallots, thinly sliced

to serve

a handful of fresh Thai basil leaves

a few fresh mint leaves

1 red chilli/chile, sliced

lime wedges

serves 4

This is Vietnamese fast food – it's slurped down in a flash but be warned that it takes time to make. It's a soothing, deeply flavoured broth bobbing with slices of beef, rice noodles and perky beansprouts and served with a bowl of Thai basil, mint, chilli/chile and lime which you add to your own taste. It is possibly one of the best dishes in the world.

Heat the sunflower oil in a large saucepan over low heat, then add the anise, lemongrass, cinnamon, coriander seeds, peppercorns, ginger and garlic. Cook gently for 1–2 minutes to release their aromas. Pour in the stock and bring to the boil. Add the coriander/cilantro sprigs and simmer for 30 minutes. Take off the heat and set aside to infuse.

Get ready a plate of condiments. Pile up the Thai basil, mint, chilli/chile and lime wedges on a plate and keep in the fridge until ready to serve.

Just before serving, cook the rice noodles in a large pan of boiling water according to the manufacturer's instructions. Drain and refresh under cold running water. Divide between 4 bowls.

Strain the stock back into the pan and add enough lime juice and fish sauce to taste. Add the beef and cook for 1 minute, or until it is just cooked through. Ladle the beef and stock onto the noodles and scatter the beansprouts and shallots over the top. Serve with the plate of condiments so everyone can season to taste.

smoked haddock
& bean soup

Smoked haddock provides that warm smoky flavour that cold wintry nights call for. Beans are a great for thickening soups and are so quick and easy to throw in. In this recipe, using both cannellini and butter beans adds to the thick and chunky texture of the soup.

4 tablespoons extra virgin olive oil

1 red onion, sliced

600 ml/2½ cups fish stock

3 dried bay leaves

finely grated zest of 1 lemon

300 g/10 oz. smoked haddock, skinned and cubed

400-g/14-oz. can cannellini beans, drained and rinsed

400-g/14-oz. can butter/lima beans, drained and rinsed

4 tablespoons crème fraîche/sour cream

salt and freshly ground black pepper

serves 4

Heat the olive oil in a large saucepan, then fry the onion. Cover and cook over low heat for 10 minutes, stirring every now and then until soft.

Pour in the stock, add the bay leaves and lemon zest and bring to a gentle simmer. Add the smoked haddock and cook for 3–4 minutes until opaque.

Put half the cannellini and half the butter beans with 200 ml/ scant 1 cup water in a blender, blend until smooth and stir into the soup. Stir in the remaining whole beans and the crème fraîche/sour cream. Season with salt. If the soup is too thick, add enough water to thin it down.

Divide the soup between 4 bowls and serve with freshly ground black pepper.

minestrone soup

4 tablespoons extra virgin olive oil, plus extra to serve

2 carrots, chopped

1 red onion, chopped

4 celery sticks, diced and leaves reserved

6 garlic cloves, sliced

2 tablespoons freshly chopped flat-leaf parsley

2 teaspoons tomato purée/paste

400-g/14-oz. can peeled plum tomatoes, chopped

1 litre/4 cups hot chicken or vegetable stock

400-g/14-oz. can borlotti beans, drained and rinsed

Parmesan rind (optional)

150 g/5 oz. cavolo nero or spring greens, shredded

100 g/3½ oz. spaghetti, broken up

grated Parmesan cheese, to serve

salt and freshly ground black pepper

serves 4–6

Parmesan rinds can be used to add a depth of flavour and saltiness to vegetable soups such as this one. Buy your Parmesan in a big chunk and keep the rinds in an airtight container in the fridge to use whenever necessary.

Heat the olive oil in a large, heavy-based saucepan, then add the carrots, onion, celery and garlic. Cover and sweat very slowly over low heat, stirring occasionally, until thoroughly softened.

Add the parsley, tomato purée and canned tomatoes and cook for 5 minutes. Pour in the stock and borlotti beans and bring to the boil. If using a Parmesan rind, add this now. Once boiling, add the cavolo nero and simmer for 20 minutes.

Add the spaghetti and cook for 2–3 minutes less than the manufacturer's instructions suggest (by the time you have ladled it into bowls it will be perfectly cooked). Taste and add seasoning if it needs it.

Divide the soup between 4–6 bowls and drizzle with extra olive oil. Serve immediately with a bowl of grated Parmesan to sprinkle over the top.

apple, parsnip & thyme soup

1 small onion, chopped

2 tablespoons olive oil

1 teaspoon mild curry powder

a few sprigs of fresh thyme

450 g/1 lb. parsnips (about 2–3), peeled and chopped

1 large tart cooking apple, such as Bramley's, peeled, cored and roughly chopped

1.25 litres/5 cups chicken or vegetable stock

1 tablespoon unsalted butter

3 heaped tablespoons crème fraîche/sour cream, plus extra to serve

croûtons, to serve (optional)

salt and freshly ground black pepper

serves 4

Parsnips have a very distinctive taste which marries well with the sweetness of apples. In this delicious soup, the two are enhanced by a pinch of spicy curry powder and some fresh thyme. Just the thing to brighten up a dreary winter's day.

Put the onions, oil, curry powder and a good pinch of salt in a large saucepan. Cook gently over low heat until the onions are soft. Add the thyme, parsnips and apple and stir well. Cook for about 5 minutes, adding a little more oil, if needed, and stirring often. Add the stock and season to taste.

Simmer gently, uncovered for about 15–20 minutes, until the parsnips are soft. Put the soup in a blender, blend until smooth, then return it to the saucepan. Taste and adjust the seasoning if necessary.

Stir in the butter and 3 heaped tablespoons crème fraîche/sour cream and mix well. Divide the soup between 4 bowls and top with croûtons, if using. Add a spoonful of crème fraîche/sour cream and serve immediately.

450 g/1 lb. squash, peeled, deseeded and cut into 1–2-cm/½ inch dice

5 tablespoons olive oil

1–2 pinches dried red chilli/hot pepper flakes, crushed (optional)

1 large onion, finely diced

2 carrots, diced

2 celery sticks, sliced

180 g/6 oz. chorizo or other spicy cooking sausage, peeled and diced

1 red chilli/chile, deseeded and finely chopped

2 garlic cloves, thinly sliced

a small of bunch of flat-leaf parsley, stalks and leaves separated, both chopped

1 teaspoon each crushed cumin seeds and coriander seeds

2 tablespoons chopped oregano or 1½ teaspoons dried

200-g/7-oz. can chopped tomatoes

400-g/14-oz. can chickpeas, drained and rinsed

1.25 litres/5 cups vegetable stock

freshly squeezed lemon juice, to taste (optional)

salt and freshly ground black pepper

serves 4–5

roasted squash, chickpea & chorizo soup

Roasting the squash adds depth of flavour and sweetness to this rustic soup, which warms the soul with its brick red and orange colours and robust, spicy flavours. Serve it with good crusty bread.

Preheat the oven to 190ºC (375ºF) Gas 5. Put the squash on a baking sheet and toss with 2 tablespoons of oil. Season with salt and pepper and sprinkle over the dried red chilli/hot pepper flakes. Roast in the preheated oven for 35–40 minutes until tender and browned, stirring once or twice.

Meanwhile, heat the remaining oil in a large saucepan and add the onion with a pinch of salt. Turn the heat to low, cover and cook gently, stirring occasionally, for 10–15 minutes until tender. Add the carrots, celery and chorizo and cook, uncovered, for a further 5–7 minutes until beginning to brown. Add the fresh chilli/chile, garlic, chopped parsley stalks and crushed spices. Stir-fry for another 4–5 minutes. Add the oregano, tomatoes, chickpeas and stock and bring to the boil. Reduce the heat and simmer gently for 10–12 minutes until the vegetables are tender. Stir in the roasted squash.

Put half the soup in a blender and blend until smooth, then return it to the saucepan and reheat. Taste and adjust the seasoning, adding more salt and/or lemon juice if necessary. Stir in the chopped parsley leaves and serve immediately with crusty bread.

spicy vegetable chowder

2 tablespoons olive oil

1 large onion, finely chopped

100 g/3–4 oz. mixed chillies/chiles deseeded and finely chopped, plus extra to garnish

3 celery sticks, chopped

225 g/7 oz. potatoes (about 2), diced

7 cm/2¾ inches fresh ginger, grated

1 small courgette/zucchini, chopped

1 fresh bay leaf

sprig of fresh thyme

600 ml/2½ cups hot vegetable stock

2 sweetcorn cobs

300 ml/1¼ cups milk

300 g/10 oz. green beans, sliced into 1.5-cm/¾-inch pieces

bunch of fresh flat-leaf parsley, finely chopped

salt and freshly ground white pepper

12 fresh basil leaves, torn, to serve

small bunch of fresh chives, snipped, to serve

serves 6

This chowder is a vegetarian dish but is in no way a mild, delicate option. Hot and robust, this dish is guaranteed to warm you up. Make it with mostly mild and medium chillies/chiles unless you like things really spicy.

Heat the oil in a large saucepan over medium heat and gently fry the onion for 1 minute. Add the chillies/chiles, celery, potatoes, ginger and courgette/zucchini, then fry for a further 2–3 minutes.

Add the bay leaf, thyme, ¼ teaspoon white pepper and hot stock and gently bring to the boil. Reduce the temperature and simmer for about 15 minutes, or until the potatoes are cooked.

Meanwhile, put the corn upright on a board and strip the kernels by running a sharp knife carefully downward. Set the kernels aside.

Remove the pan from the heat, discard the bay leaf and thyme sprig. Transfer the soup to a blender and blend until smooth. Return the soup to the pan.

Stir in the milk, then add the beans and reserved corn kernels. Mix thoroughly and simmer for about 12–15 minutes until the beans and corn are tender. Add the parsley and season to taste with salt and white pepper.

Divide the chowder between 6 bowls and garnish with the fresh basil, chives and a little more of the chopped chillies/chiles.

Here you'll find a selection of comfort food snacks, perfect for sharing. Choose from quesadillas oozing with melted cheese, sweet and sticky glazed ribs, fluffy baked potatoes and buttermilk-marinated fried chicken.

hearty snacks

sole goujons

2 tablespoons olive oil

2 tablespoons unsalted butter

200 g/4 cups fresh, fine breadcrumbs

1 tablespoon freshly chopped flat-leaf parsley

2 teaspoons freshly chopped thyme

finely grated zest of 1 lemon

1 teaspoon Spanish smoked paprika

450 g/1 lb. skinless sole fillets

4 tablespoons plain/all-purpose flour

2 eggs, beaten

sea salt and freshly ground black pepper

to serve

tomato ketchup

tartare sauce

oven-cooked french fries

lemon wedges

a baking sheet, lined with baking parchment

serves 4

In this take on fancy fish and chips, the breadcrumbs are fried until golden in a little olive oil and butter – this way the fish can be baked in the oven rather than deep-fried. Serve with oven-cooked fries, ketchup and tartare sauce.

Preheat the oven to 220°C (425°F) Gas 7.

Heat the oil and butter in a large frying pan, add the breadcrumbs and, stirring constantly, cook until golden. Tip the crumbs into a large bowl, add the chopped herbs, lemon zest and paprika and season well with salt and black pepper. Let cool.

Cut each sole fillet into strips roughly 2–3 cm/1 inch wide.

Tip the flour into one shallow dish and the beaten eggs into another. Taking one piece of fish at a time, coat it first in the flour, then the beaten eggs, then the breadcrumbs. Arrange the goujons on the prepared baking sheet and bake in the preheated oven for about 10 minutes, or until cooked through.

Serve immediately with tomato ketchup, tartare sauce, oven-cooked french fries and lemon wedges.

pepper beef quesadilla

This filling is a real crowd pleaser and the seasoning can be varied to keep it as mild, or as spicy, as desired.

2 tablespoons vegetable oil

1 onion, diced

1 red bell pepper, diced

1 yellow bell pepper, diced

1 teaspoon ground cumin

1 teaspoon dried oregano

½ teaspoon paprika

1 fresh red or green chilli/chile

2 garlic cloves, crushed

450 g/1 lb. beef mince/ground beef

1 teaspoon fine sea salt

220 g/1 cup canned chopped tomatoes

8 large flour tortillas

150 g/1½ cups grated Cheddar or Monterey Jack cheese

to serve

sour cream

spring onions/scallions, sliced

diced tomatoes

pitted black olives, sliced

serves 4–6

Preheat the oven to 120°C (250°F) Gas ½.

Heat 1 tablespoon of the oil in a frying pan set over medium–high heat. Add the onion and peppers and cook for 5–8 minutes, stirring occasionally, until golden. Add the cumin, oregano, paprika, chilli/chile and garlic and cook for 1 minute further. Add the beef and salt and cook for 5 minutes until browned. Stir in the tomatoes and simmer until slightly reduced and thickened. Taste and adjust the seasoning.

To assemble the quesadillas, spread a quarter of the beef mixture on 4 of the tortillas. Sprinkle each with a quarter of the cheese and top with another tortilla.

Heat the remaining oil in a non-stick frying pan set over medium heat. When hot, add a quesadilla, lower the heat and cook for 2–3 minutes until golden on one side and the cheese begins to melt. Turn over and cook the other side for 2–3 minutes. Transfer to a heatproof plate and keep warm in the preheated oven while you cook the rest.

To serve, top each quesadilla with sour cream, spring onions/scallions, diced tomatoes and sliced olives. Cut into wedges and serve immediately.

huevos rancheros

This dish is hot! If you prefer it slightly milder, reduce the amount of fiery green chilli appropriately.

½ tablespoon olive oil

8 slices of back or streaky/fatty bacon, finely chopped

1 large onion, finely chopped

1 garlic clove, crushed

4 hot green chillies/chiles, finely chopped

1 mild red chilli/chile, deseeded and finely chopped

4 tomatoes, skinned and roughly chopped

½ teaspoon sea salt

¼ teaspoon freshly ground black pepper

8 eggs

4 plain 20-cm/8-inch flour tortillas

a spicy salsa, to serve

serves 4

Heat the oil in a frying pan and gently fry the bacon until almost cooked. Drain off all but 1 teaspoon of the fat.

Add the onion and garlic to the pan and cook, allowing to lightly brown. Add the chillies/chiles, tomatoes, salt and pepper, stir well and cover. Bring to the boil, reduce the heat and simmer for about 20 minutes, stirring frequently.

Meanwhile, fry or poach the eggs to your taste and gently warm the tortillas in a frying pan or warm oven, or under the grill/broiler.

To serve, place 2 eggs per person on a warmed tortilla and liberally spoon the salsa over the eggs. Eat immediately!

creole seafood burritos

25 g/2 tablespoons butter

1 onion, chopped

2 garlic cloves, finely sliced

½ teaspoon ground Ancho or other dried chilli

1 teaspoon Creole spice blend

225 g/8 oz. cooked/lump white crabmeat

125 g/4 oz. peeled cooked prawns/shrimp, chopped

100 g/1 cup grated Gruyère cheese

6 plain 25-cm/10-inch flour tortillas

sea salt and freshly ground black pepper

to serve

sour cream

a spicy salsa

shredded lettuce leaves

serves 6

This is a wonderfully simple dish that is great for the whole family. It is mild and child friendly but can easily be made 'dad friendly' with the simple addition of some hot salsa or even a few finely chopped Ring of Fire chillies at the end of cooking.

Heat the butter in a large frying pan, then gently fry the onion for 3 minutes. Add the garlic, chilli and Creole spice blend and cook for 10 minutes over low heat until soft, stirring to prevent the mixture from sticking.

Reduce the heat and stir in the crab and prawns/shrimp. Gently heat through and then season with salt and pepper to taste. Stir in the grated Gruyère cheese.

To serve, put a generous tablespoon of the seafood mixture onto a tortilla. Add, in equal quantities, a dollop of sour cream and one of the salsa. Add a little shredded lettuce for crunch. Fold the tortilla up over the bottom of the mixture and roll the sides around the seafood mixture. Leave the top open if you are eating immediately. Repeat with the remaining tortillas and serve.

Tip: If you don't like too much heat, try serving these with some mild guacamole instead of the spicy salsa, and some finely chopped celery for extra crunch.

patatas bravas

400 g/14 oz. new waxy potatoes, scrubbed

1 tablespoon olive oil

2 garlic cloves, crushed

1 hot red chilli/chile, deseeded and finely chopped

2–3 large, ripe tomatoes, roughly chopped

a pinch of sweet smoked paprika (pimentón dulce)

½ teaspoon paprika

a pinch of saffron strands

1 teaspoon dried wild oregano

2 tablespoons olive oil
(or 1 olive oil and 1 chilli oil)

sea salt flakes and freshly ground black pepper

serves 4 as a tapas dish

Known worldwide as a great tapas dish, this classic Spanish recipe takes all the flavours of rural Spain and combines them to wonderful effect. As with the majority of simple dishes, the success of this recipe is defined by the quality of the ingredients that go into it. Fresh potatoes and garlic, ripe tomatoes and chilli and good-quality olive oil make this a delight to make as well as eat!

Cut the potatoes into 2-cm/¾-inch pieces. Put them in a large saucepan of lightly salted boiling water, cover and bring back to the boil. Cook until they are cooked through but still firm. Drain and pat dry with kitchen paper/paper towels.

Put the 1 tablespoon oil in a small frying pan set over medium heat and fry the garlic and chilli for about 1 minute. Add the tomatoes and cook for a further 2 minutes. Add both types of paprika, the saffron and oregano. Stir and cook for a further 5–10 minutes until the flavours have fully mingled and the tomatoes have softened. Remove from the heat and cover.

Put the 2 tablespoons oil in a large frying pan over medium–high heat and fry the now-dry cubes of potato until golden brown and crispy. Season these with salt and pepper and serve topped with the spicy tomato sauce.

sticky orange beef lettuce wraps

400 g/14 oz. beef fillet

1 tablespoon light soy sauce

4 tablespoons cornflour/cornstarch

vegetable oil, for frying

2 Little Gem/Bibb lettuces, leaves separated

lime wedges, to serve

sauce

2 garlic cloves, crushed

1 teaspoon finely grated fresh ginger

3 tablespoons dark soy sauce

grated zest of 1 large orange

75 ml/5 tablespoons freshly squeezed orange juice

4 tablespoons honey

1 generous tablespoon tomato ketchup

serves 4–6

Sweet, sticky and finger-lickin' good, these orange-glazed beef strips make a great sharing dish. Serve them with crisp lettuce leaves to make the perfect fingerfood wrappers.

Put the beef in the freezer for 20 minutes, or until quite firm, then remove and cut into thin strips. Toss the beef in the soy sauce, then put in a freezer bag with the cornflour/cornstarch. Seal the bag and give it a good shake so that all the beef strips are evenly coated.

Pour a 2-cm/¾-inch depth of oil in a wok and heat until hot. Add the beef in small batches, separating the strips with tongs to stop them sticking together. Cook for 2–3 minutes, or until browned and crisp. Remove with a slotted spoon and leave to drain on kitchen paper/paper towels.

To make the sauce, pour away most of the oil from the wok, leaving about ½ tablespoon. Heat this gently, then add the garlic and ginger and stir-fry for 1 minute. Add the remaining sauce ingredients and bring to the boil. Leave it to bubble away briskly for 3 minutes, or until thickened.

Return the beef to the wok and cook for a few minutes until the sauce is sticky and clings to the beef. Remove from the heat.

Divide the beef between 4–6 plates and serve with lettuce leaves and lime wedges. Wrap the beef in the leaves and enjoy!

cajun-spiced, souffléd baked potatoes

A freshly baked potato is always a hearty, comforting snack. You can vary the fillings to your taste, experimenting with different spices or cheeses: the possibilities are endless.

2 large baking potatoes, scrubbed

1 tablespoon butter

1 generous teaspoon Dijon mustard

2 teaspoons Cajun spice blend

2 spring onions/scallions, chopped

1 mild green chilli/chile, deseeded and chopped

100 g/1 cup grated mature/sharp Cheddar cheese, plus extra for sprinkling

1 egg, lightly beaten

sea salt and freshly ground black pepper

serves 2

Preheat the oven to 200°C (400°F) Gas 6.

Pierce the potato skins several times with a fork, then place the potatoes directly on a shelf in the preheated oven. Bake until the flesh is soft enough to scrape out, and the skins are crispy enough to retain their shape – about 50–70 minutes, depending on the size of the potatoes. Set the potatoes aside until cool enough to handle. Leave the oven on.

Cut the potatoes in half lengthways, spoon the insides into a large bowl and mash the potato until it is fairly lump-free. Add the butter, mustard, Cajun spice blend, spring onions/scallions, cheese and most of the chilli/chile and stir together until well mixed, then check the seasoning. Quickly mix the beaten egg through the mashed potato mixture, then spoon the mixture back into the skins.

Sprinkle some extra grated cheese over the filled potatoes and top with the reserved chilli/chile. Place the potatoes onto a small baking dish and return to the oven for a further 15–20 minutes or until the cheese starts to brown. The egg will cause the potatoes to rise slightly in a sort of scaled-down soufflé effect, giving them an unexpected lightness.

spiced fried chicken

3 skinless chicken breasts

150 ml/⅔ cup buttermilk

100 g/¾ cup plain/all-purpose flour

1 generous teaspoon baking powder

1 generous teaspoon sea salt flakes

½ teaspoon ground cayenne pepper

½ teaspoon Spanish smoked paprika

¼ teaspoon ground coriander

¼ teaspoon garlic powder

a pinch of ground allspice

½ teaspoon dried oregano

freshly ground black pepper

sunflower oil, for frying

serves 4

Marinating chicken in buttermilk tenderizes the meat and makes these little chicken nuggets really juicy. These are perfect for a snack, or serve with chilli-spiced potato wedges and creamy coleslaw for a hearty meal.

Cut each chicken breast into 5 or 6 strips. Place in a ceramic dish and coat with the buttermilk. Cover with clingfilm/plastic wrap and chill for at least 2 hours.

Remove the chicken from the buttermilk and pat off any excess with kitchen paper/paper towels. Combine the flour, baking powder, salt flakes, spices, oregano and some black pepper in a bowl. Toss the chicken pieces in the seasoned flour and set aside on baking parchment for 10 minutes.

Pour 3–4 tablespoons sunflower oil in a frying pan. Set over medium heat and add one-third of the chicken pieces. Cook until golden and crispy. Drain on kitchen paper/paper towels and repeat with the remaining 2 batches of chicken.

sticky spare ribs

1 kg/2 lbs. short or loin pork ribs/
country-style pork spare ribs

4 garlic cloves, crushed

2 tablespoons grated fresh ginger

4 tablespoons (clear) honey

2 tablespoons soy sauce

2 tablespoons hoisin sauce

2 tablespoons sweet chilli sauce

2 tablespoons tamarind paste

¼ teaspoon Chinese five-spice
powder

a large roasting dish

serves 4-6

**Finger-licking good! You'll need a pile of napkins for these.
Serve with ice-cold beers.**

Place the ribs in a saucepan of water, bring up to the boil and
simmer for 5–10 minutes, then drain.

Mix the remaining ingredients together in a large bowl, add the
ribs and stir thoroughly to coat. Let cool and allow to marinate
for about 30 minutes.

Preheat the oven to 190°C (375°F) Gas 5.

Tip the ribs and marinade into a large roasting dish, cover with
foil and cook on the middle shelf of the preheated oven for
about 20 minutes. Remove the foil, turn the ribs over, basting
them with the marinade, and cook for another 20 minutes until
sticky and browned all over. Allow to rest for a couple of minutes
before serving with plenty of napkins.

corned beef hash

The British invented bubble and squeak as a clever way to use leftover boiled dinner (boiled beef brisket, potato and cabbage). Americans dropped the cabbage and renamed it corned beef hash – a savoury, hearty dish.

3 baking potatoes (about 700 g/1½ lbs.), peeled and diced

3 tablespoons butter

1 onion, diced

1 garlic clove, finely chopped

300 g/10½ oz. cooked corned beef brisket, diced

½ teaspoon Tabasco Sauce

1 tablespoon pure vegetable oil

4 eggs

serves 4

Boil the potatoes in salted water for 6 minutes, drain and put in a large bowl.

Heat 1 tablespoon of the butter in a large, heavy frying pan. Add the onion, garlic and corned beef. Season and sauté for 5 minutes. Pour the mixture into the bowl with the potatoes, add the Tabasco and mix well.

Add the remaining butter to the frying pan. Pour the potato mixture into it and press everything down firmly. Cover with a heavy lid or plate that will fit just inside the pan to weight the mixture down. Cook over medium heat for 10 minutes. Turn the mixture over in batches and cook for 10 minutes on the other side. The meat should be brown and crisp. Keep cooking and turning if it isn't. Make 4 indentations in the potatoes and crack an egg into each. Place a fitted lid over the pan and cook until the eggs are done. Alternatively, in a separate non-stick frying pan, heat 1 tablespoon vegetable oil and fry the eggs. Place one fried egg on top of each serving of corned beef hash. You can also poach the eggs instead of frying them.

Here are some particularly comforting bowlfuls that can be eaten lazily with just a fork or chopsticks. Recipes include velvety risottos and the ultimate mac 'n' cheese, or turn up the heat with Asian and Mexican classics.

rice & noodles

wild mushroom & leek risotto

Warm, hearty and satisfying, risotto is the perfect comfort food. This dish is full of earthy winter flavours. Try to buy 'trompettes de la mort' mushrooms if you can find them, but if not use porcini or charterelles.

900 ml/3¾ cups vegetable stock

4 tablespoons extra virgin olive oil, plus extra for the parsley oil

1 large onion, finely chopped

2 leeks, chopped

6 garlic cloves, finely chopped

350 g/1¾ cups Arborio or Carnaroli rice

125 ml/½ cup dry white wine

200 ml/¾ cup cream

300 g/10 oz. mixed wild mushrooms

3 tablespoons finely chopped parsley

salt and freshly ground black pepper

serves 6–8

Heat the vegetable stock in a saucepan and keep it at just under boiling point, ready to add into the risotto.

Heat 3 tablespoons oil in a heavy-based pan, add the onion and leeks and cook gently over low heat until soft and translucent, but not coloured. Add 5 of the chopped garlic cloves, turn up the heat and stir for 1 minute. Add the rice, stirring frequently until the grains are coated in oil and beginning to turn translucent.

Pour in the wine and season with a pinch of salt. Gradually add the hot stock a ladleful at a time, adding another ladle as soon as the liquid has been absorbed by the rice.

When the stock is finished, stir in the cream and some pepper. Season to taste, then turn down the heat.

In a separate pan, warm 1 tablespoon oil over medium–high heat. Add the mushrooms and fry for 1–2 minutes until the mushrooms have softened and coloured a little.

Add the mushrooms to the risotto. Make a quick parsley oil by combining the chopped parsley with the remaining chopped garlic clove and as much oil as you like. Drizzle over the risotto and serve immediately.

ingredients

50 g/1¾ oz. anchovy fillets in brine or olive oil, drained

3 tablespoons extra virgin olive oil

2 garlic cloves, thinly sliced

1 red chilli/chile, deseeded and finely chopped

500 g/1 generous lb. plum tomatoes, skinned

50 g/⅓ cup capers

40 g/¼ cup green olives, pitted and chopped

2 tablespoons tomato purée/paste

100 g/⅔ cup black or Kalamata olives, pitted and chopped

salt and freshly ground black pepper

cooked spaghetti, or other pasta noodle such as tagliatelle, to serve

serves 2

puttanesca pasta sauce

This authentic Italian pasta dish is guaranteed to transport you to sunnier climes. It is robust, salty and very satisfying; quick to make, but with wonderfully well-balanced flavours. It captures the sunshine of southern Italy perfectly – delicious served with a bottle of full-bodied Italian red wine.

Rinse the anchovy fillets under cold water for a few moments to desalt or remove excess oil. Pat the fillets dry on some kitchen paper/paper towels. Chop roughly.

Heat the oil in a saucepan and fry the garlic and chilli/chile for about 3–4 minutes until statring to brown. Add the anchovies and continue to fry for about 1 minute, or until they begin to break down. Add the chopped tomatoes, capers, green olives and tomato purée/paste. Stir thoroughly. Turn the heat down and simmer gently, uncovered, for 20 minutes.

Add the black olives and cook for a further 5 minutes. Season only at the end of cooking, as there is a quite a lot of salt in the anchovies and the capers.

Serve with spaghetti and a salad of dolcelatte, tomato, basil and herby salad leaves. The sauce should be robust, strong and salty, and is perfect with a bottle of full-bodied Italian red wine.

bibimbap

400 g/14 oz. pork belly, chopped into thin 2.5-cm/1-inch pieces

400 g/2 cups short grain brown rice

vegetable, sunflower or rapeseed oil

2 carrots, cut into thin strips

toasted sesame oil

dark soy sauce

agave syrup or runny honey

150 g/5 oz. oyster or shiitake mushrooms

150 g/5 oz. beansprouts

3 onions, sliced

200 g/6½ oz. spinach leaves

4 eggs

2 spring onions/scallions, finely chopped

black sesame seeds

Sauce

4 tablespoons gochujang paste

4 tablespoons toasted sesame oil

4 tablespoons dark soy sauce

2 garlic cloves, crushed

2 tablespoons agave syrup

serves 4

Served in a steaming hot stone bowl, the presentation of this traditional Korean dish is just as exciting as the punchy chilli/chile and sesame flavours inside. Good-quality ingredients make a world of difference for a truly authentic Korean taste, and gochujang, which is a slightly sweet chilli/chile paste, is well worth seeking out in Asian food stores.

To make the sauce, mix together all the ingredients. Pour half the sauce over the pork belly in a bowl, cover and marinate in the fridge for at least 1 hour, or more if you have time.

Cook the rice according to the manufacturer's instructions and keep warm. While the rice is cooking, heat 1 tablespoon oil in a pan or wok and stir-fry the carrots until beginning to soften. Add ½ teaspoon sesame oil, soy sauce and agave syrup. Cook for 1 minute over high heat, then set aside on a plate. Cook the mushrooms, beansprouts, onions, and spinach separately, seasoning at the end.

In the same pan you used for the vegetables, stir-fry the marinated pork (with the sauce it was sitting in) until cooked through. The sauce should reduce down a little with the heat.

In a separate pan, fry the 4 eggs however you like them. Divide the hot rice between 4 bowls and top with individual piles of vegetables and meat, finishing off with the egg in the middle and a sprinkling of spring onions/scallions and sesame seeds.

Serve with the remaining sauce, adding as much or as little as you like.

a bowl of red

Chunks of tender steak and puréed dried chillies/chiles make this mouth-watering beef chili extra special. Spicy and filling, it is just the right dish for a mid-week pick-me-up. Serve with cooked rice, grated cheese and fresh coriander/cilantro.

1 kg/2¼ lbs. braising steak, cut into 4-cm/1¾-inch chunks

1 bottle of beer

4 dried whole chillies/chiles, deseeded

6 tablespoons olive oil

2 large onions, roughly chopped

6 garlic cloves, finely chopped

2 x 400-g/14-oz. cans peeled plum tomatoes

75 ml/¼ cup cider vinegar

60 g/¼ cup brown sugar

1 tablespoon Spanish paprika

1 tablespoon chilli/chili powder

3 tablespoons cumin seeds, toasted and ground

400-g/14-oz. can kidney, borlotti or pinto beans, drained and rinsed

salt and freshly ground pepper

cooked rice, grated cheese, chopped red onion and fresh coriander/cilantro leaves, to serve

serves 4–6

Put the beef in a medium bowl, pour over the beer and leave to marinate for 30 minutes. Drain, reserving the liquid and pat the beef dry with kitchen paper/paper towels. Toast the chillies/chiles for 30 seconds in a dry sauté pan then pour boiling water over and soak for 15 minutes or until soft. Drain and put in a food processor with the beer. Purée until fine and set aside.

In a large saucepan, heat 2 tablespoons of the olive oil. Season the meat and sear in batches until evenly browned. Remove from the pan and set aside. Add the remaining olive oil and sauté the onions and garlic for 5 minutes. Put the meat back in the pan and pour the chilli/chile mixture over.

Purée the tomatoes in a food processor and add to the pan. Add the cider vinegar, brown sugar, paprika, chilli/chili powder and cumin, and season. Cook, partially covered with a lid, for 1 hour over low heat or until the meat is very tender. Add the beans in the last 5 minutes of cooking to warm through. Serve in small bowls with cooked rice, chopped red onion, grated cheese and coriander/cilantro leaves.

thai-style golden seafood noodle salad

While this fresh, colourful salad is a great summer dish, it is so vibrant and cheery that it may be served up in colder months to brighten up gloomy days. The Thai ingredients here can be found in most Asian stores.

200 g/14 oz. dried vermicelli rice noodles

1 tablespoon ground turmeric

500 g/1 lb. large cooked prawns/shrimp, peeled and deveined

1 red (bell) pepper, deseeded and thinly sliced

3 spring onions/scallions, thinly sliced on the angle

1 large green chilli/chile, thinly sliced

a small bunch of fresh coriander/cilantro, leaves and some stalks roughly chopped and a few small sprigs reserved to garnish

3 tablespoons Thai fish sauce

2 tablespoons freshly squeezed lime juice

1 teaspoon sugar

serves 4

Put the noodles in a large, heatproof bowl.

Put 1.5 litres/6 cups water in a saucepan over high heat. Add the turmeric and bring to the boil. As soon as the water boils, pour it over the noodles and leave for 5–6 minutes, until the noodles are cooked. Rinse and drain well.

Transfer the noodles to a separate bowl with the prawns/shrimp, red pepper, spring onions/scallions, chilli/chile and coriander/cilantro.

Put the fish sauce, lime juice and sugar in a small bowl and whisk with a fork to combine. Pour over the noodles. Sprinkle with the coriander/cilantro sprigs and serve immediately.

300 g/10½ oz. sirloin beef or fillet, trimmed of fat and very thinly sliced

300 g/10½ oz. fresh medium egg noodles

1½ tablespoons peanut oil

3 spring onions/scallions, finely chopped, white and green parts kept separately

170 g/1½ cups choy sum (or pak-choi), chopped, stalks and leaves kept separately

1 red chilli/chile, thinly sliced, to garnish (optional)

Marinade

1½ tablespoons dark soy sauce

½ tablespoon Chinese rice wine

½ teaspoon sugar

1 garlic clove, crushed

1 teaspoon finely grated fresh ginger

2 teaspoons cornflour/cornstarch

Sauce

2 tablespoons oyster sauce

200 ml/⅔ cup chicken stock

1 tablespoon light soy sauce

1 tablespoon dark soy sauce

2 teaspoons cornflour/cornstarch

Serves 2

beef chow mein

Chow mein is a classic noodle stir-fry that should be part of every keen cook's repertoire. Treat this recipe as a basic guide to which you can add your own touches. Try varying the vegetables and replacing the beef with chicken or even tofu.

Put the beef in a bowl, add all the marinade ingredients, mix well and set aside.

Bring a saucepan of water to the boil. Add the noodles and blanch for 2–3 minutes. Drain and rinse under cold running water. Set aside.

Combine all the sauce ingredients in a bowl and set aside.

Heat 1 tablespoon of the oil in a wok or large frying pan until hot. Add the marinated beef in 2 batches and stir-fry over high heat for 2–3 minutes, or until well sealed all over. Remove the beef from the wok and set aside.

Heat the remaining oil in the wok, then add the white parts of the spring onions/scallions and stir-fry for just 30 seconds. Add the stalks of the choy sum and stir-fry for 2 minutes. Pour in the sauce and bring to the boil. Leave to bubble for 1 minute, then return the beef to the wok and stir through.

Stir the drained noodles into the wok, then cook for 1–2 minutes, or until the noodles are tender. Divide the chow mein between 2 bowls, garnish with the remaining spring onions/scallions and the chilli/chile, if using, and serve immediately.

wicked mac & cheese

Mac and cheese is a firm comfort food favourite. Here it's given a modern makeover with gourmet cheeses like mascarpone and Parmesan, and a touch of garlic. The crisp topping rounds out the texture, making it live up to its name.

60 g/½ cup fresh, chunky breadcrumbs

1 tablespoon olive oil

2 tablespoons butter

1 garlic clove, finely chopped

1 teaspoon dry mustard

3 tablespoons plain/all-purpose flour

500 ml/2 cups milk

125 ml/½ cup mascarpone

130 g/1 cup mature Cheddar cheese, grated

60 g/½ cup grated Parmesan cheese

350 g/12 oz. macaroni noodles or other tube pasta, such as rigatoni

serves 4

Preheat the oven to 200°C (400°F) Gas 6.

Spread the breadcrumbs on a baking sheet, drizzle with the oil and season. Bake for 6 minutes, remove and set aside.

Melt the butter in a medium saucepan. Add the garlic and mustard and sauté for 1 minute before adding the flour. Whisk constantly over medium heat until it forms a paste. Gradually whisk in the milk and turn up the heat. Bring to the boil, whisking constantly. Turn the heat down to low and simmer for 10 minutes. Remove from the heat and add the mascarpone, Cheddar and half of the Parmesan.

Boil the pasta in salted water until just al dente, drain and mix with the cheese sauce. Season and spoon the mixture into a baking dish. Top with the breadcrumbs and the remaining Parmesan. Bake for 20 minutes until golden. Let sit for 5 minutes before serving.

triple tomato & basil risotto

The risotto is full of the intense flavour of tomatoes, added in three ways: passata to the stock; sun-dried tomatoes adding their caramel flavour deep in the risotto; then tiny plum tomatoes, roasted to perfect sweetness.

450 g/1 lb. whole baby plum tomatoes

4 tablespoons olive oil

1 litre/4 cups hot vegetable stock

500 ml/2 cups passata (Italian sieved tomatoes)

115 g/1 stick unsalted butter

1 onion, finely chopped

8 pieces sun-dried tomatoes (not in oil), chopped

400 g/2 cups risotto rice,

150 ml/⅔ cup light red wine

50 g/½ cup freshly grated Parmesan cheese

4 tablespoons chopped fresh basil

salt and freshly ground black pepper

to serve

extra basil leaves

freshly grated Parmesan cheese

serves 4

Preheat the oven to 200°C (400°F) Gas 6.

Put the plum tomatoes in a roasting pan and pour over the olive oil. Mix well to coat and season with salt and pepper. Roast in the preheated oven for 20 minutes or until beginning to brown. Remove from the oven and set aside.

Pour the stock and passata into a saucepan, stir well, then heat to a gentle simmer. Melt half the butter in a large saucepan and add the onion and sun-dried tomatoes. Cook gently for 10 minutes until soft and translucent. Add the rice and stir until well coated and heated through. Pour in the wine and boil hard until it has reduced and almost disappeared. Remove from the heat.

Return the risotto to the heat and add the stock, a large ladle at a time, stirring gently until each ladle has almost been absorbed by the rice. Continue until all the stock has been used up and the rice is tender and creamy, but the grains still firm.

Season to taste with salt and pepper, beat in the remaining butter, the Parmesan and chopped basil. You may like to add a little more hot stock at this stage to loosen the risotto – it should be quite wet. Cover and let rest for a couple of minutes, then divide between 4 bowls. Cover the surface with the roasted tomatoes and any juices. Add the basil leaves and serve immediately with grated Parmesan cheese.

roasted garlic risotto

Roasting a big batch of garlic makes sure that you will always have some in the refrigerator for adding to soups or even spreading on toast or bruschetta. You can keep roasted garlic in the fridge for up to 1 week.

20 large garlic cloves, peeled

75 ml/⅓ cup extra virgin olive oil, plus extra for basting

4–6 large thick slices goat cheese with rind

4–6 small sprigs of rosemary, plus extra to serve

1.5 litres/6 cups chicken stock

1 red onion, finely chopped

2 tablespoons chopped fresh rosemary

500 g/2⅓ cups risotto rice

200 g/8 oz. soft mild goat cheese (without rind)

50 g/½ cup freshly grated Parmesan cheese

salt and freshly ground black pepper

serves 4–6

Preheat the oven to 180°C (350°F) Gas 4.

Put the garlic, 2 tablespoons of oil, salt and pepper in a mixing bowl and toss well. Seal the coated garlic inside a piece of foil and roast for 20 minutes, then turn over and roast for 10 minutes more. Reserve 8 cloves to use.

Put the sliced goat cheese on a baking sheet lined baking parchment. Brush with olive oil and put a rosemary sprig on each one. Sprinkle with pepper and set aside. Preheat the grill/broiler.

Put the stock in a saucepan and keep at a gentle simmer. Heat the remaining olive oil in a saucepan. Add the onion and cook gently for 5 minutes. Add the roasted garlic and half the chopped rosemary. Cook for a further 5 minutes, then stir in the rice until well coated and heated through. Begin adding the stock, a large ladle at a time, stirring gently until each ladle has almost been absorbed by the rice. Halfway through cooking the risotto, grill/broil the sliced goat cheese until browned. Continue adding stock until the rice is tender and creamy, but the grains still firm. Stir in the soft cheese and remaining rosemary.

Taste and season well with salt and pepper and beat in the Parmesan cheese. Cover and let rest for a couple of minutes, then divide between 4–6 bowls. Add a slice of grilled/broiled goat cheese to each serving and top with a sprig of rosemary.

Choose from spicy sausage rolls or chicken pot pies – lovers of buttery pastry will not be disappointed! Or try a simple-to-assemble bake, designed to go from oven to table, such as the perfect lasagne or a mouthwatering moussaka.

pies & oven bakes

corned beef & sweet potato pasties

800 g/1 lb. 12 oz. ready-made shortcrust pastry dough

2 tablespoons sunflower oil

1 onion, finely chopped

1 large orange-fleshed sweet potato, diced

2 tablespoons spicy mango chutney or sweet chilli sauce

2 tablespoons chopped fresh thyme or lemon thyme

450 g/1 lb. canned corned beef, chilled and diced

1 egg, beaten, to glaze

salt and freshly ground black pepper

a 20-cm/8-inch dinner plate

a baking sheet lined with non-stick baking parchment

makes 6 large pasties

These pasties are almost like corned beef hash in pastry. Use orange-fleshed sweet potatoes, which have a lovely smooth texture. The fresh thyme is essential, and be sure to season with plenty of black pepper.

Roll out the pastry on a lightly floured surface and cut out 6 rounds, using the plate as a guide.

Heat the oil in a sauté or large frying pan and add the onion. Cook over medium heat for 5 minutes until beginning to soften. Add the sweet potato and cook, stirring from time to time, for 10 minutes or until just tender. Stir in the chutney or sweet chilli sauce and thyme and leave to cool. Once cold, fold in the corned beef and season well.

Divide the mixture between the 6 pastry circles and crimp the edges together to seal in the filling. Brush with the beaten egg and chill for 30 minutes.

Preheat the oven to 200°C (400°F) Gas 6.

Arrange the chilled pasties on the prepared baking sheet, make a little steam hole in each one and bake in the preheated oven for 20–30 minutes until the pastry is golden brown. Remove from the oven and serve hot or transfer to a wire rack to cool.

bacon, egg & parsley pie

This is the British equivalent of a French Quiche Lorraine, but with a double crust, which keeps the filling from drying out. It is perfect for a simple meal served with a peppery watercress salad.

400 g/14 oz. ready-made shortcrust pastry dough

4 large eggs, plus 2 egg yolks

300 ml/1 ¼ cups double/heavy cream or crème fraîche

3 tablespoons roughly chopped fresh parsley

a pinch of ground mace or freshly grated nutmeg

250 g/9 oz. smoked dry-cure, rindless streaky/fatty bacon, roughly chopped

1 egg, beaten, to glaze

freshly ground black pepper

a 20-cm/8-inch pie plate or loose-based cake pan

serves 4–6

Roll out two-thirds of the pastry on a lightly floured surface and use it to line the pie plate. Roll out the remaining pastry to a round that will easily cover the pie and slide it onto a baking sheet. Chill both the lined pie plate and the lid pastry for at least 20 minutes.

Preheat the oven to 220°C (425°F) Gas 7 and set a heavy baking sheet on the middle shelf.

Put the whole eggs, egg yolks, cream, parsley and mace or nutmeg into a blender or liquidizer and blend until smooth and a pale green colour. Alternatively, use a stick blender.

Scatter the bacon over the base of the pastry and pour over the cream mixture. Brush the edges of the pastry with the beaten egg and lay the pastry lid over the pie. Crimp the edges together to seal. Brush the surface with beaten egg, and make a couple of steam holes in the top of the pie. Decorate the top with pastry trimmings if you like.

Bake in the preheated oven for 15 minutes, then reduce the oven temperature to 180°C (350°F) Gas 4 and bake for a further 45 minutes or until golden in colour and set. Remove from the oven and cool for 10 minutes before removing from the pan to cool on a wire rack. Serve warm or at room temperature.

glorious golden fish pie

350 g/12 oz. raw shell-on tiger prawns/shrimp

700 ml/3 cups milk

1 onion, chopped

1 bay leaf

2 peppercorns

450 g/1 lb. fresh sustainable white fish fillets (such as cod, haddock pollack), skin on

450 g/1 lb. undyed smoked haddock or cod fillet, skin on

75 g/5 tablespoons butter

75 g/½ cup plus 1 tablespoon plain/all-purpose flour

4 tablespoons chopped fresh parsley

salt and freshly ground black pepper

saffron and dill mash

1.3 kg/3 lbs. floury potatoes, peeled

a large pinch of saffron strands soaked in 3 tablespoons hot water

75 g/5 tablespoons butter

250 ml/1 cup milk

3 tablespoons chopped fresh dill

a 1.5-litre/quart oval pie dish

serves 4–6

The secret of a well-flavoured moist and juicy fish pie is not to overcook the fish. You can make the mash without the saffron, but try it for a treat – it looks and tastes wonderful.

Peel the shells from the prawns/shrimp. Put the shells in a saucepan with the milk, onion, bay leaf and peppercorns. Bring to the boil then lower the heat and simmer for 10 minutes. Turn off the heat and set aside to infuse.

Lay the white and smoked fish fillets, skin side up, in a roasting pan. Strain the infused milk into the pan and and simmer on the hob/stovetop for 5–7 minutes until just opaque. Lift the fish fillets out of the milk and transfer to a plate. When the fillets are cool enough to handle, pull off the skin and flake the fish into large pieces, removing any bones as you go. Transfer to a large bowl and add the shelled prawns/shrimp.

Melt the butter in a small saucepan set over medium heat, stir in the flour and gradually add the flavoured milk from the roasting pan. Whisk well and simmer gently for 15 minutes until thick and a little reduced. Taste and season with salt and pepper. Stir in the parsley and pour the sauce over the fish. Carefully mix everything together, then transfer the mixture to the pie dish and let cool.

Preheat the oven to 180°C (350°F) Gas 4.

Boil the potatoes in salted water until soft, drain well and mash. Beat in the saffron and its soaking water (if using), butter, milk and dill. When the fish mixture is cold, spoon over the golden mash, piling it up on top. Bake in the preheated oven for 30–40 minutes or until the potato is golden brown and crispy. If it fails to brown enough, finish it off under a medium grill/broiler. Serve immediately.

chicken pot pie

55 g/4 tablespoons butter

1 large leek, trimmed and sliced

2 carrots, peeled and diced

450 g/1 lb. skinless, boneless chicken breast, cubed

about 8 leaves of fresh tarragon, chopped

3 tablespoons chopped fresh parsley

150 g/generous 1 cup fresh or frozen peas

250 ml/1 cup crème fraîche or double/heavy cream

500 g/1 lb. 2 oz. ready-made all-butter puff pastry dough

2 egg yolks, lightly beaten with a pinch of salt, to glaze

salt and freshly ground black pepper

4 x 250-ml/1-cup ovenproof dishes

serves 4

This pie is a quick comfort food, so the traditional white sauce has been replaced with crème fraîche.

Melt the butter in a medium saucepan and add the leek and carrots. Cook for about 10 minutes or until they are both soft and cooked through. Add the chicken, stir well and cook for about 10 minutes until the chicken is cooked through. Stir in the tarragon and parsley, followed by the peas and crème fraîche. Bring to the boil, then remove from the heat and set aside.

Roll out the pastry on a lightly floured surface and cut 4 round discs at least 2.5 cm/1 inch wider than the diameter of your ovenproof dishes.

Spoon the chicken filling evenly into the dishes, brush the edges of the dishes with a little beaten egg yolk and top each with a pastry round. Press the pastry firmly down onto the edges of the dishes to seal. (You don't need to make a hole in the lid of these – the puff pastry wants to rise up into a dome.) Brush with beaten egg yolk and chill for at least 30 minutes.

Preheat the oven to 200°C (400°F) Gas 6.

Remove the pies from the fridge, brush with more beaten egg yolk (thinned down with a little water or milk if necessary) to build up a nice glaze, then set them on a large baking sheet. Bake the pies in the preheated oven for about 20 minutes or until the pastry tops are puffed and golden brown and the pies are bubbling hot inside.

pasta & cherry tomato pies

These classic Scottish pies always have a 1-cm/½-inch rim of pastry extending above the filling to provide a space for additions such as mashed potatoes or baked beans. Served freshly baked from the oven.

110 g/4 oz. dried pasta shapes (such as macaroni or fusilli)

40 g/3 tablespoons butter

2½ tablespoons plain/all-purpose flour

a pinch of cayenne pepper

a pinch of English mustard powder

350 ml/1½ cups milk

100 g/1½ cups grated mature/sharp Cheddar cheese

30 cherry tomatoes, halved

50 g/⅔ cup grated Parmesan

salt and freshly ground black pepper

hot water crust pastry

450 g/3⅔ cups plain/all-purpose flour

1 teaspoon salt

2 eggs, beaten

160 g/⅔ cup lard

100 ml/6 tablespoons milk

6 x 10-cm/4-inch straight-sided ramekins, jars or chef's rings

makes 6

Start making the pie crusts the day before. Sift the flour and salt into a mixing bowl. Make a well in the centre and pour in the eggs, flicking a little flour over the top. Put the lard, milk and 6 tablespoons water into a saucepan and slowly bring to the boil (do not let it boil before the lard is melted). Pour the boiling liquid into the flour and mix. Tip out onto a floured surface and knead lightly until smooth and no longer streaky. Wrap in clingfilm/plastic wrap and chill for at least 30 minutes. While the pastry is chilling, cover the chosen pie moulds with clingfilm/plastic wrap.

Divide the pastry dough into 6 pieces. On a floured surface, roll out each piece thinly, drape over the upturned base of each mould and smooth to fit. Don't worry about uneven edges – these will be trimmed off later. Set on a tray and chill for 30 minutes. When firmly set, use a sharp knife to trim the pastry on each one to 5 cm/2 inches deep. Carefully ease the pie crusts out of the moulds and pull out the clingfilm/plastic wrap. Set the pie crusts on a tray and leave to dry out in a cool dry place for 24 hours.

Preheat the oven to 200ºC (400ºF) Gas 6. Cook the pasta according to the package instructions. While the pasta is cooking, melt the butter in a medium saucepan and add the flour, cayenne pepper and mustard. Cook, stirring, for 1 minute. Remove from the heat, pour in the milk and whisk in well. Return to the heat and stir until boiling. Simmer, stirring all the time, for 2 minutes. Drain the pasta well and stir into the sauce. Season to taste and stir in the Cheddar. Set aside and leave to cool until tepid.

Spoon the pasta sauce into the dried pie crusts, leaving enough of a rim of pastry projecting above to hold the tomatoes. Pile the tomato over the surface of the pies and sprinkle with the Parmesan. Stand the pies in a shallow baking pan and bake in the preheated oven for 10–15 minutes to set the pastry. Reduce the oven temperature to 180ºC (350ºF) Gas 4 and bake for a further 20 minutes, or until golden and bubbling.

butternut squash & corn bread pudding

In this delicious vegetarian bake, the sweetness of the squash and corn go well with the creamy, cheesy bread 'pudding' part. In place of the baguette, you could save up the ends from sliced loaves. And any kind of cheese can be used here, as can a combination of cheeses, so it's a good way to use up odds and ends. Serve with a mixed salad.

1 tablespoon olive oil

1 large onion, halved and thinly sliced

375 ml/1½ cups milk

225 ml/scant 1 cup single/light cream

3 eggs, beaten

a small bunch of fresh chives, snipped

leaves from a small bunch of fresh parsley, finely chopped

1 baguette, cut into ½-cm/¼-inch slices

300 g/2 cups (sweet)corn kernels, canned or frozen

about 500 g/1 lb. peeled and sliced butternut squash

100 g/1 cup grated mature/sharp Cheddar cheese

salt and freshly ground black pepper

a 30 x 20 cm/12 x 8-inch baking dish, very well buttered

serves 4–6

Preheat the oven to 190°C (375°F) Gas 5.

Heat the oil in a large frying pan. Add the onion and cook over low heat for 3–5 minutes, until soft. Season lightly and set aside.

Combine the milk, cream and eggs in a small bowl and whisk to combine. Season with 1½ teaspoons salt. Add the chives and parsley, mix well and set aside.

Arrange half the baguette slices in the prepared baking dish in a single layer; you may need to tear some to cover all the space. Put half of the onion slices on top, then scatter over half of the (sweet)corn. Arrange half of the squash slices evenly on top and sprinkle with half of the cheese. Repeat one more time (bread, onion, (sweet)corn, squash, cheese). Stir the milk mixture and pour it evenly all over the pudding.

Cover the dish tightly with foil and bake in the preheated oven for 20 minutes. Remove the foil and continue baking for about 30–40 minutes, until golden. Serve immediately.

- 2–3 tablespoons olive oil
- 1 onion, finely chopped
- ½ teaspoon dried oregano
- ½ teaspoon dried thyme
- 130 g/5 oz. white mushrooms, coarsely chopped
- 4 garlic cloves, crushed
- ¼ teaspoon dried red chilli/hot pepper flakes
- 125 ml/½ cup dry white or red wine
- 2 x 400-g/14-oz. cans chopped tomatoes
- 410-g/14-oz. can artichoke hearts, drained and sliced
- 50 g/½ cup pitted black olives, sliced
- a pinch of sugar
- 400 g/14 oz. dried tube pasta, such as penne or rigatoni
- 150 g/6 oz. provolone, cubed

béchamel sauce

- 50 g/3 tablespoons unsalted butter
- 35 g/¼ cup plain/all-purpose flour
- 600 ml/2½ cups hot milk
- 3–4 tablespoons freshly grated Parmesan cheese
- salt and freshly ground black pepper

a 30 x 20-cm/12 x 8-inch baking dish

serves 4

artichoke, mushroom & olive pasta bake

Here is a great pasta bake, packed with flavour. Provolone is a smoked Italian cheese, but almost any cheese can be used so do experiment.

Heat 1 tablespoon of the oil in a large frying pan. Add the onion and cook over low heat for about 5 minutes, until soft. Stir in the oregano, thyme and mushrooms and cook for 2–3 minutes more, adding a little more oil if required. Stir in the garlic and chilli/hot pepper flakes and season with salt. Cook for 1 minute, then add the wine. Cook for 1 minute more, then add the tomatoes, olives and artichokes. Add the sugar, season and stir, then simmer for about 15 minutes. Taste and adjust the seasoning if necessary.

Preheat the oven to 200°C (400°F) Gas 6. Cook the pasta according the packet instructions until just al dente. Drain and set aside.

For the béchamel, melt the butter in a saucepan set over low heat. Add the flour and cook, stirring, for 1 minute. Pour in the hot milk, whisking continuously, and simmer until the mixture thickens. Season, stir in 2 tablespoons of the Parmesan and set aside.

To assemble, spread a small amount of the tomato mixture over the bottom of the baking dish and add 1 tablespoon of the oil. Arrange about one-third of the cooked pasta in a single layer on the bottom. Top with half of the remaining tomato mixture and spread evenly. Cover with another layer of pasta (using half of the remaining amount). Spoon over half of the béchamel and spread evenly. Top with the provolone, spacing the pieces evenly. Spoon the remaining tomato mixture on top. Top with the remaining pasta and béchamel. Sprinkle with the remaining Parmesan. Bake in the preheated oven for about 30–40 minutes, until browned. Serve immediately.

root vegetable gratin

There is something very satisfying and tranquil about preparing this recipe. So if the thought of peeling and slicing these vegetables puts you off, think again. It sounds perhaps more daunting than it really is; but you will be done in no time, and it will be well worth the effort. This is a very simple dish, very impressive and hugely delightful. Serve with a cheese platter, crusty bread and a green salad.

3 small turnips (about 375 g/ 13 oz.), peeled, halved and very thinly sliced

½ a celeriac (about 325 g/11 oz.), peeled, halved and very thinly sliced

½ a swede (about 450 g/1 lb.), peeled, halved and very thinly sliced

650 g/1½ lbs. waxy potatoes, peeled, halved and very thinly sliced

225 ml/scant 1 cup double/heavy cream

100 g/6 tablespoons crème fraîche or sour cream

250 ml/1 cup milk

125 g/1¼ cups grated Gruyère or medium Cheddar cheese

salt and freshly ground black pepper

a 30 x 20-cm/12 x 8-inch baking dish, very well buttered

serves 4–6

Preheat the oven to 200°C (400°F) Gas 6.

Put all the vegetable slices in a large bowl and toss gently to combine. Set aside.

Combine the cream, crème fraîche and milk in a small saucepan and heat just to melt the crème fraîche. Stir well and season with salt and pepper.

Arrange half of the vegetables slices in the prepared baking dish. Sprinkle with a little salt and one-third of the cheese, then pour over one-third of the cream mixture. Top with the rest of the vegetable slices, the remaining cheese and another sprinkle of salt, then pour over the remaining cream mixture. Transfer the dish to the preheated oven and bake for 1–1½ hours, until browned on top. Serve immediately.

baked rigatoni with mozzarella

3 tablespoons olive oil

1 small onion, diced

1 carrot, finely diced

2–3 celery sticks, from the inner section, with leaves, diced

1 small red, yellow or orange (bell) pepper, deseeded and diced

100 g/4 oz. mushrooms, diced

3 garlic cloves, finely chopped

125 ml/½ cup dry white or red wine

½–1 teaspoon dried red chilli/hot pepper flakes, to taste

½ tablespoon fresh thyme leaves or 1 teaspoon dried thyme

a large handful of fresh parsley or basil leaves, finely chopped

400-g/14-oz. can chopped tomatoes

a 700-g bottle/3 cups passata (Italian sieved tomatoes)

a pinch of sugar

500 g/1 lb. dried rigatoni

500 g/1 lb. mozzarella, sliced

sea salt and freshly ground black pepper

a 30 x 20-cm/12 x 8-inch baking dish, well oiled

serves 4–6

Very simple to make, with virtuous quantities of vegetables, this is a good way to eat well with minimal effort. The important thing is to chop all the vegetables into dice of the same size, to allow them to nestle inside the pasta shapes.

Heat the oil in a large saucepan, add the onion and cook over low heat for 3–5 minutes, until soft. Add the carrot, celery and pepper. Season and cook for 2–3 minutes. Stir in the mushrooms and garlic and cook for 1 minute more. Add the wine and cook for 1 minute more. Stir in the chilli/hot pepper flakes, thyme, parsley, tomatoes, passata and sugar. Season generously and stir. Reduce the heat and simmer, uncovered, for 20–30 minutes. Taste and adjust the seasoning if necessary.

Meanwhile, cook the pasta according to the packet instructions until al dente. Drain well and set aside.

Preheat the oven to 200°C (400°F) Gas 6.

Combine the cooked pasta and the vegetable sauce and mix well. Spread half the pasta in the prepared dish evenly. Top with half of the mozzarella. Top with the remaining pasta in an even layer and arrange the remaining mozzarella slices on top.

Bake in the preheated oven for 25–30 minutes, until the cheese melts and bubbles. Serve immediately.

mashed potato pie with bacon, leeks & cheese

1 kg/2¼ lbs. floury potatoes, peeled

2 tablespoons olive oil

1 onion, finely chopped

2 small leeks, thinly sliced

80 g/½ cup diced thick-sliced bacon or pancetta

2 tablespoons butter

250 ml/1 cup milk or single cream (or a bit of both)

1 egg, beaten

a large handful of fresh parsley leaves, chopped

a pinch of paprika

90 g/⅔ cup grated firm cheese, such as Gruyère

salt and freshly ground black pepper

a 24-cm/10-inch round baking dish, well buttered

serves 4–6

This is a great way to make a meal out of simple mashed potato. Bacon, leeks and cheese make a particularly perfect trio, but you can add just about anything to this versatile dish. You should have onion at the very least, and cheese of some sort, and a green herb for a bit of colour.

Halve or quarter the potatoes depending on their size; they should be about the same to cook evenly. Put them in a large saucepan, add sufficient cold water to cover, salt well and bring to the boil. Simmer for about 20 minutes, until tender and easily pierced with a skewer.

Meanwhile, heat the oil in a frying pan set over low heat. Add the onion and leeks and cook gently for about 10 minutes, until soft. Add the bacon and cook for 3–5 minutes, until just browned. Season with salt and set aside.

Preheat the oven to 190°C (375°F) Gas 5.

Drain the potatoes and mash coarsely, mixing in the butter and milk. Season well and add the egg. Stir to combine thoroughly.

Stir in the leek mixture, parsley, paprika and half the cheese. Transfer to the prepared dish and spread evenly. Sprinkle over the remaining cheese and bake in the preheated oven for 35–45 minutes, until well browned. Serve immediately.

moussaka

This take on the classic Greek dish omits the potatoes and has a yogurt topping in place of the traditional béchamel sauce. This improves over time so is best made a day in advance, refrigerated and baked when ready to serve.

1 onion, chopped

4–5 tablespoons olive oil

500 g/1 lb. minced/ground lamb

2 garlic cloves, finely chopped

½ teaspoon ground allspice

¼ teaspoon ground cinnamon

2 teaspoons dried oregano

125 ml/½ cup red wine

2 x 400-g/14-oz. cans chopped tomatoes

1 bay leaf, plus extra to garnish

a pinch of sugar

3 aubergines/eggplants, sliced into 1-cm/½-inch rounds

salt and freshly ground black pepper

topping

350 ml/1½ cups Greek yogurt

2 eggs, beaten

150 g/6 oz. feta, crumbled

a large handful of fresh mint leaves, chopped

3 tablespoons freshly grated Parmesan

a 30 x 20-cm/12 x 8-inch baking dish

serves 6

Combine the onion and 1 tablespoon of the oil in a large frying pan. Cook the onion for about 3–5 minutes, until soft. Add the lamb, season well and cook, stirring, for about 5 minutes, until browned. Add the garlic, allspice, cinnamon and oregano and cook for 1 minute. Add the wine and cook for 1 minute more. Add the tomatoes, bay leaf and sugar and mix well. Let simmer gently, uncovered, while you prepare the aubergines/eggplants.

Preheat the oven to 200°C (400°F) Gas 6.

Heat a few tablespoons of the oil in a large non-stick frying pan. Add the aubergine/eggplant slices in a single layer and cook to brown slightly. Using tongs, turn and cook the other sides, then transfer to kitchen paper/paper towels to drain. Work in batches, adding more oil as necessary, until all the slices are browned.

In a bowl, combine the yogurt, eggs and feta and mix well. Season well with salt and pepper and stir in the mint. Set aside.

To assemble the moussaka, spread half of the lamb mixture over the bottom of the baking dish. Top with half of the aubergine/eggplant slices. Repeat once more, then spread the yogurt mixture smoothly on top. Sprinkle with the Parmesan and decorate with bay leaves. Bake in the preheated oven for about 40–50 minutes, until golden and bubbling. Serve immediately.

baked large pasta shells

1 onion, finely chopped

2 tablespoons olive oil

2 large garlic cloves, crushed

40 g/1½ oz. pancetta, finely chopped

300 g/10 oz. minced/ground beef

2 tablespoons tomato purée/paste

125 ml/½ cup red wine

400 g/14 oz. can chopped tomatoes

225 ml/1 cup vegetable stock

½ teaspoon dried oregano

1 teaspoon (caster) sugar

200 g/7 oz. conchiglioni rigati pasta (large pasta shells)

2 tablespoons freshly grated Parmesan

1 generous tablespoon freshly grated Cheddar cheese

salt and freshly ground black pepper

fresh basil leaves, to serve

a medium ovenproof dish

serves 4

All the work for this dish can be done ahead of time: the ragù and tomato sauce can be made, the pasta cooked and filled, and the dish completely assembled. Sprinkle the cheese over the top and heat in a moderate oven when needed.

For the ragù, gently fry half the onion in a saucepan with half the oil. Add half the garlic and all the pancetta and continue to cook for a couple of minutes until tender but not coloured. Add the beef and brown quickly. Add half the tomato purée/paste and all the wine and cook for 30 seconds, then add half the chopped tomatoes and half the stock. Bring to the boil, then reduce the heat to a very gentle simmer and cook for about 1 hour, or until the beef is tender and the sauce thick.

To make the tomato sauce, heat the remaining oil in another pan, add the remaining onion and fry gently until tender. Add the remaining garlic, cook for 30 seconds, then add the remaining tomato paste, chopped tomatoes, stock and oregano. Bring to the boil, reduce the heat to a gentle simmer and cook for about 30 minutes, or until reduced slightly. Taste and add a pinch of sugar if needed and plenty of salt and black pepper.

Preheat the oven to 190°C (375°F) Gas 5.

Cook the pasta in a large pan of salted water until al dente, following the package instructions. Drain, refresh under cold running water, then drain well again.

Pour the tomato sauce into an ovenproof dish. Fill each pasta shell with the ragù and arrange over the tomato sauce. Scatter a mixture of grated Parmesan and Cheddar all over the pasta and bake in the preheated oven for about 20 minutes, or until bubbling hot. Scatter basil over the baked dish and serve immediately.

creamy pancetta & onion tart

1 tablespoon olive oil

170 g/6 oz. diced pancetta

3 onions, sliced

1 large garlic clove, crushed

1 teaspoon (caster) sugar

2 sprigs of fresh thyme

375 g/12½ oz. ready-made
all-butter puff pastry dough

250 g/1 cup crème fraîche

salt and freshly ground
black pepper

2 solid baking sheets

serves 4

A delicious combination of sweet onions, salty pancetta and tangy crème fraîche, all gently infused with thyme and cooked on a buttery puff pastry base. Serve simply with a salad.

Preheat the oven to 200°C (400°F) Gas 6 and place one of the baking sheets on the middle shelf to heat up.

Heat the olive oil in a large frying pan over medium heat, add the pancetta and cook until crisp. Remove from the pan with a slotted spoon and drain on kitchen paper/paper towels. Add the sliced onions to the pan and cook for about 10 minutes, stirring occasionally until they start to colour. Add the garlic, sugar and leaves from the thyme sprigs and cook for a further minute to caramelize the onions. Remove from the heat, stir in the pancetta and let cool slightly.

Roll out the puff pastry dough on a lightly floured work surface. Keep rolling until it's big enough to trim into a rectangle about 30 x 20 cm/12 x 8 inches. Using the tip of the knife, score a border 2 cm/1 inch from the edge without cutting all the way through the dough. Carefully lift the dough onto the second baking sheet and slide into the preheated oven on top of the hot baking sheet. Cook for 7 minutes, then remove from the oven.

Season the crème fraîche with salt and pepper and spread half of it over the tart base. Season the onion and pancetta mixture with salt and pepper too and spread over the crème fraîche. Dot the remaining crème fraîche over the filling and return to the oven for a further 20 minutes, or until the pastry is golden and the filling is bubbling. Serve hot or warm, cut into individual portions.

cassoulet

675 g/4 cups dried butter/lima beans, or other white beans

500 g/1 lb. smoked Italian pancetta, fat bacon or belly pork, in a piece

4 tablespoons olive oil

4 boneless duck breasts, halved crossways, or chicken legs or thighs

750 g/1½ lbs. fresh Toulouse sausages or Italian coarse pork sausages, cut into 3 pieces each

2 medium onions, chopped

1 large carrot, chopped

4–6 large garlic cloves, crushed

3 bay leaves

2 teaspoons dried thyme

2 whole cloves

3 tablespoons tomato purée

12 sun-dried tomatoes in oil, drained and coarsely chopped

75 g/1½ cups fresh white breadcrumbs (ciabatta is good)

50 g/4 tablespoons butter

salt and freshly ground black pepper

serves 6–8

This hearty dish from south-west France is big and filling and will become a firm family favourite. It reheats very well and is a boon for entertaining large numbers without fuss.

The night before, put the beans in a very large bowl, cover with plenty of cold water (to cover them by their depth again) and let soak for several hours. Note: if you are short of time, use canned beans.

The next day, drain the beans well and tip into a large saucepan. Cover with fresh water, bring to the boil, then simmer for about 1 hour or until just cooked. Drain well (reserving the cooking liquid).

Trim and discard the rind from the pancetta, and cut the flesh into large pieces. Heat 2 tablespoons of the oil in a frying pan, brown the pieces in batches and transfer to a plate. Heat the remaining oil in the pan, add the duck breasts and fry skin side down until the skin is golden. Transfer to the same plate as the pancetta. Brown the sausages in the same way and add to the plate. Add the onions to the pan, then the carrot, garlic, bay leaves, dried thyme, cloves, tomato purée and sun-dried tomatoes. Cook for 5 minutes until softening.

To assemble the dish, put half the beans in a large, deep casserole. Add an even layer of all the meats, then the onion and tomato mixture. Season well with salt and pepper. Cover with the remaining beans, then add enough reserved hot cooking liquid until the beans are almost covered. Sprinkle evenly with breadcrumbs and dot with butter. Bake the cassoulet in a preheated oven at 180°C (350°F) Gas 4 for about 1 hour until a golden crust has formed. Serve warm straight out of the dish.

polenta pizza

2 teaspoons bouillon stock powder

200 g/1 ⅓ cups polenta/yellow cornmeal

grated zest and freshly squeezed juice of 1 lemon

6 garlic cloves, crushed

salt and freshly ground black pepper

1 tablespoon fresh thyme leaves

1 head of rainbow or Swiss chard

extra virgin olive oil

200 g/7 oz. girolle/golden chanterelle mushrooms

1 tablespoon freshly chopped parsley

1 egg

a bunch of fresh marjoram

a large baking sheet, oiled

serves 6

This delicious wheat-free pizza soaks up all the juices from the toppings. It makes a fantastic lunch or dinner dish to share with friends.

Bring 1 litre/4 cups water to the boil and add the bouillon powder. Reduce the heat and pour in the polenta/cornmeal, whisking all the time until blended. Reduce the heat to its lowest setting, add half the lemon zest and juice, 4 of the crushed garlic cloves, the thyme and a good pinch of salt and pepper and gently cook, stirring occasionally, for about 45 minutes or until the polenta pulls away from the side of the pan and is very thick.

Meanwhile, bring another pan of water to the boil. Add 1 teaspoon salt and boil the chard for about 3–4 minutes until the thick part is just tender, but not limp. If the root end of the chard is very thick, separate it from the leaves and boil each part separately until just tender. Remove, drain and season with some salt and oil. In the meantime, don't forget to stir the polenta!

Heat 2 tablespoons oil in a pan over medium–high heat. Fry the mushrooms for about 2 minutes or until just golden and tender. Add 1 of the garlic cloves and stir for 30 seconds to release the garlic flavour, but don't let it burn. Transfer to a bowl, toss with the parsley and season with salt, the remaining lemon zest and juice, and some olive oil.

When the polenta is ready, transfer to the prepared baking sheet and spread out to a thickness of about 2 cm/¾ inch. Allow to cool and firm up for 30 minutes.

Preheat the grill/broiler. Scatter the mushrooms and chard over the top of the polenta. Crack an egg carefully into the middle and grill/broil for 4–5 minutes or until the egg is cooked.

Meanwhile, pull the leaves off the marjoram stalks and finely chop. Mix the chopped leaves with the last crushed garlic clove and mix with enough oil to form a loose marjoram oil.

Remove the polenta from the grill/broiler and slide onto a board. Drizzle the marjoram oil over the top and serve immediately.

aubergine & tomato gratin

2 red onions, sliced

10 cherry tomatoes – as ripe and red as you can find

extra virgin olive oil

salt and freshly ground black pepper

balsamic vinegar

3 aubergines/eggplants, topped, tailed and cut into 1-cm/½-inch slices

a handful of fresh basil leaves

100 ml/6 tablespoons soy cream/creamer

serves 4–6

The velvety creaminess of this dairy-free dish just screams 'bad for you', so it is such a joy to be able to scream back 'no it's not!' Aubergine/eggplant can be quite bland if not really encouraged with good seasoning, so this is the perfect dish for them – the tomatoes, oil, non-dairy cream and herbs really bring it to life.

Preheat the oven to 200°C (400°F) Gas 6.

Toss the onions and tomatoes with some oil, salt and a drizzle of balsamic vinegar in an ovenproof dish. Roast in the preheated oven for about 15 minutes or until the skins of the tomatoes crack open and the onions are beginning to caramelize. Leave the oven on.

Meanwhile, heat a saucepan over medium heat. Using a pastry brush, coat the aubergine/eggplant slices with oil on both sides. Fry in the hot pan until golden brown on both sides and beginning to get soft. Transfer to a dish and give them a generous drizzle of oil. Season well with salt and a little pepper.

Layer the aubergine/eggplant slices in a casserole dish with the tomatoes, onions and basil leaves (reserving some for serving). Pour the cream over, drizzle over some oil and bake in the oven for 15–20 minutes until bubbling and golden on top.

Remove from the oven. Tear the remaining basil leaves and scatter over the top of the dish. Serve immediately.

dukkah & harissa sausage rolls

500 g/1 lb. minced/ground lamb

1 teaspoon smoked paprika

1 teaspoon ground cinnamon

4 tablespoons harissa or sun-dried tomato purée/paste

500 g/1 lb. 2 oz. ready-made puff pastry dough

1 egg, beaten

salt and freshly ground black pepper

dukkah

2 tablespoons sesame seeds

2 tablespoons pine nuts

1 teaspoon coriander seeds

1 teaspoon cumin seeds

a baking sheet, lightly oiled

serves 4

The plain old sausage roll gets a bit of an exotic make-over here with an Egyptian spice blend called dukkah.

Preheat the oven to 200°C (400°F) Gas 6.

To make the dukkah, put the sesame seeds, pine nuts, coriander seeds, cumin seeds and a pinch of salt in a mortar. Bash them with the pestle until crushed, but try to maintain a little texture so they are not pounded into a powder.

Put the lamb, paprika, cinnamon and harissa in a mixing bowl with some seasoning and mix with your hands, squelching it all together until thoroughly blended together.

Roll out the pastry on a lightly floured work surface until you have a rectangle measuring 25 x 60 cm/10 x 24 inches (and about 3 mm/⅛ inch thick). Cut into 4, at 15-cm/6-inch intervals. This will give you 4 rectangles, each 25 x 15 cm/10 x 6 inches. Spoon about 4 tablespoons of the sausage mixture onto each rectangle. Brush a little beaten egg along one short side. Fold the pastry over from one short side to meet the other short side. Press the folded edges together to seal and crimp by pressing down with a fork. Leave the other 2 sides of the rolls open so that you can still see the filling.

Repeat to make 3 more rolls. Brush them with more beaten egg and sprinkle the dukkah over the top. Transfer to the prepared baking sheet and bake in the preheated oven for 25–35 minutes, until golden and cooked through.

lasagne al forno

about 12 sheets fresh lasagne

about 50 g/½ cup freshly grated
Parmesan cheese

béchamel sauce

75 g /3 oz. pancetta or dry-cure
smoked bacon in a piece

100 g/4 oz. chicken livers

50 g/3 tablespoons butter

1 onion, finely chopped

1 carrot, chopped

1 celery stick, trimmed and finely
chopped

250 g/9 oz. minced/ground beef

2 tablespoons tomato purée/paste

100 ml/⅓ cup dry white wine

200 ml/¾ cup beef stock or water

freshly grated nutmeg

salt and freshly ground
black pepper

béchamel sauce

75 g/5 tablespoons butter

55 g/⅓ cup plain/all-purpose flour

about 500 ml/2 cups milk

salt, to taste

*a deep 20 x 25-cm/8 x 10-inch
baking dish, buttered*

serves 4–6

**Everyone's favourite, this classic comfort food dish is layered
with satisfying pasta, rich meat ragu and a creamy sauce.**

To make the ragù, cut the pancetta into small cubes. Trim the
chicken livers, removing any fat or gristle. Cut off any discoloured
bits, which will be bitter if left on. Coarsely chop the livers.

Melt the butter in a saucepan, add the pancetta and cook for
2–3 minutes until browning. Add the onion, carrot and celery
and brown these too. Stir in the beef and brown until just
changing colour, but not hardening – break it up with a wooden
spoon. Stir in the chicken livers and cook for 2–3 minutes.
Add the tomato purée/paste, mix well and pour in the wine and
stock. Season well with nutmeg, salt and pepper. Bring to the
boil, cover and simmer very gently for as long as you can –
2 hours if possible.

For the béchamel sauce, melt the butter in a saucepan. When
foaming, add the flour and cook over gentle heat for about
5 minutes without letting it brown. Have a balloon whisk ready.
Slide off the heat and add all the milk at once, whisking very
well. When all the flour and butter have been amalgamated and
there are no lumps, return to the heat and slowly bring to the
boil, whisking all the time. When it comes to the boil, add salt
and simmer gently for 2–3 minutes.

Spoon one-third of the meat sauce into the prepared baking
dish. Cover with 4 sheets of lasagne and spread with one-third
of the béchamel. Repeat twice more, finishing with a layer
of béchamel covering the whole top. Sprinkle with Parmesan
cheese and bake in a preheated oven at 180°C (350°F)
Gas 4 for about 45 minutes until brown and bubbling. Let
stand for 10 minutes to settle and firm up before serving.

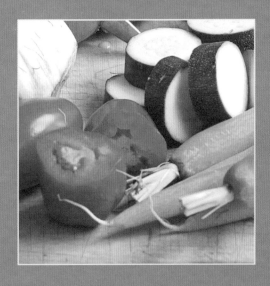

It's easier than you think to make your own exotic dishes at home. Using fresh, widely available ingredients, these one-pot recipes for favourite dishes from India, China, Vietnam and Morocco simply can't be beaten for flavour.

curries & stews

2 tablespoons vegetable oil

1 kg/1¼ lbs. braising steak, cut into bite-size pieces

1 garlic clove, crushed

1 large shallot, sliced

2-cm/1-inch piece of fresh ginger, peeled and grated (about 1 tablespoon)

750 ml/3 cups beef stock

125 ml/½ cup Chinese rice wine

125 ml/½ cup hoisin sauce

¼ teaspoon ground cumin

1 star anise

1 fresh red chilli/chile, sliced

freshly squeezed juice of 1 tangerine (or ½ an orange)

1 teaspoon runny honey

4–6 pak-choi/bok-choy

your choice of noodles, to serve

Serves 4

asian beef braise with pak-choi

A different kind of beef stew, this recipe has flavours of the Orient but is easy to make at home with ordinary Western utensils. Serve this with any kind of Oriental noodle – egg noodles will do the trick, or try something unusual like Japanese soba noodles or thick Ho Fun noodles.

Heat the oil in a large saucepan. Add the steak and cook until browned. Transfer to a plate, season with salt and set aside.

Add the garlic, shallot and ginger to the saucepan and cook, stirring constantly for 1 minute. Add the stock, rice wine, hoisin sauce, cumin, star anise, chilli/chile, tangerine juice and honey. Stir to blend and bring to the boil. Return the steak to the saucepan, reduce the heat and simmer very gently, uncovered, for 1–1½ hours, until the meat is tender. Taste and adjust the seasoning.

Core the pak-choi. Cut the white part into 1.5 cm/½-inch slices; leave the greens large or cut in half. Add the white part to the saucepan, increase the heat and cook until just tender, 3–4 minutes. Add the greens and cook until just wilted, only about 2–3 minutes more. Serve immediately with cooked noodles of your choice.

500 g/1 lb. boned leg of lamb, cut into bite-size pieces

4 tablespoons sunflower oil

1 onion, finely chopped

1 tablespoon ground coriander

1 teaspoon ground cumin

1 teaspoon chilli/chili powder

1 teaspoon ground turmeric

225 g/8 oz. canned chopped tomatoes

marinade

4 garlic cloves, crushed

1 teaspoon grated fresh ginger

150 ml/⅔ cup plain yogurt

6 tablespoons freshly chopped coriander/cilantro leaves

rice

4 tablespoons sunflower oil

2 teaspoons cumin seeds

1 onion, thinly sliced

6 cloves

10 black peppercorns

4 cardamom pods

1 cinnamon stick

225 g/1¾ cups basmati rice

1 teaspoon saffron strands

3 tablespoons warm milk

an ovenproof casserole dish with a tight-fitting lid, lightly buttered

serves 4

lamb biryani

This festive Indian one-pot rice and lamb preparation is the perfect combination of fluffy rice and tender pieces of lamb.

To make the marinade, combine the garlic, ginger, yogurt and coriander/cilantro in a glass bowl. Add the lamb and rub the marinade in. Cover and marinate in the fridge for 4–6 hours.

Heat the sunflower oil in a heavy-based pan, add the onion and cook for 12–15 minutes, until lightly golden. Add the marinated lamb and cook over high heat for 15 minutes, stirring often. Stir in the ground coriander, cumin, chilli powder, turmeric and tinned tomatoes, season well and bring to the boil. Reduce the heat to low and simmer gently for 30 minutes, or until the lamb is tender and most of the liquid has been absorbed. Set aside.

Prepare the rice. Heat the sunflower oil in a heavy-based pan. Add the cumin seeds, onion, cloves, peppercorns, cardamom pods and cinnamon and stir-fry for 6–8 minutes. Add the rice and stir-fry for 2 minutes. Pour in 400 ml/1⅔ cups water and bring to the boil. Cover and simmer gently for 6–7 minutes. Set aside. Mix the saffron and milk and set aside.

Preheat the oven to 180°C (350°F) Gas 4.

Put a thin layer of the meat mixture in the casserole and cover with half the rice. Drizzle over half the saffron mixture. Top with the remaining lamb mixture and cover with the remaining rice. Drizzle over the remaining saffron mixture, cover the dish with foil, then cover with the lid. Bake in the preheated oven for 30 minutes. Remove from the oven and let rest, still covered, for 30 minutes before serving.

lamb rogan josh

This slow-cooked lamb stew from Kashmir in north India is perfect for hassle-free entertaining as it almost cooks itself!

2 tablespoons sunflower oil

800 g/1¾ lbs. boneless lamb shoulder, cut into large bite-size pieces

2 large onions, thickly sliced

3 garlic cloves, crushed

2 teaspoons grated fresh ginger

2 cassia barks or cinnamon sticks

2 teaspoons Kashmiri chilli powder

2 teaspoons paprika

6 cardamom pods

4 tablespoons medium curry paste

400-g/14-oz. can chopped tomatoes

6 tablespoons tomato purée/paste

1 teaspoon sugar

400 ml/⅔ cup lamb stock

4–6 potatoes, peeled and left whole

freshly chopped coriander/cilantro leaves, to garnish

whisked plain yogurt, to drizzle

serves 4

Heat half the sunflower oil in a large, heavy-based casserole dish and cook the lamb, in batches, for 3–4 minutes, until evenly browned. Remove with a slotted spoon and set aside.

Add the remaining oil to the dish and add the onions. Cook over medium heat for 10–12 minutes, stirring often, until soft and lightly browned.

Add the garlic, ginger, cassia, chilli powder, paprika and cardamom pods. Stir-fry for 1–2 minutes, then add the curry paste and lamb. Stir-fry for 2–3 minutes, then stir in the tinned tomatoes, tomato purée/paste, sugar, stock and potatoes. Season well and bring to the boil. Reduce the heat to very low (using a heat diffuser if possible) and cover tightly. Simmer gently for 2–2½ hours, or until the lamb is meltingly tender.

Remove from the heat and garnish with the coriander/cilantro and a drizzle of yogurt.

lamb & bean tagine with buttered couscous

1.25 kg/2¾ lbs. boneless shoulder of lamb or shoulder chops, cut into large chunks

2 teaspoons ground cinnamon

2 teaspoons ground cumin

½ teaspoon hot chilli/chili powder

1 teaspoon ground turmeric

a pinch of saffron strands

½ teaspoon ground white pepper

2 tablespoons olive oil

3 onions, chopped

3 garlic cloves, and crushed

600 ml/2½ cups hot lamb stock

150 g/1 cup dates, pitted

200 g/1 cup broad/fava beans, podded

fresh coriander/cilantro, to garnish

buttered couscous

175 g/1⅓ cups couscous

325 ml/1⅓ cups boiling lamb stock

50 g/3 tablespoons butter, diced

a tagine or large casserole dish

serves 4

A tagine is a Moroccan stew of slow-cooked meat, often made sweet with the addition of dried fruit and served with warm buttery couscous. What's more, it has all the warming spices you crave when there's a chill in the air.

Put the lamb in a large bowl and toss with the cinnamon, cumin, chilli/chili powder, turmeric, saffron and white pepper. Heat the olive oil in a tagine or casserole dish over high heat, then add half the lamb. Cook for a few minutes, stirring occasionally, until the lamb is evenly browned. Tip into a bowl, add more oil to the tagine dish and brown the remainder of the lamb. Put all the lamb back in with the onions, garlic, stock and a large pinch of salt. Bring the mixture to the boil, cover with a lid and reduce the heat. Simmer gently for 1 hour.

Add the dates to the tagine and simmer for a further 20 minutes.

Add the broad/fava beans and simmer for a further 10 minutes. The tagine should have been cooking for 1½ hours and the meat should be so tender that it falls apart easily.

When the tagine is ready, put the couscous in a large bowl, pour over the stock and add the butter. Cover with a plate and set aside to allow the couscous to swell for 6–7 minutes.

Fluff up the couscous with a fork and serve with the tagine. Garnish with coriander/cilantro.

tarka dhal

25 g/2 tablespoons butter

2 tablespoons sunflower oil

1 white onion, thinly sliced

1 teaspoon yellow mustard seeds

½ teaspoon fenugreek seeds

½ teaspoon ground ginger

3 garlic cloves, finely chopped

125 g/⅔ cup red split lentils

350 g/1½ cups creamed tomatoes or passata (Italian strained tomatoes)

freshly squeezed juice of 1 lemon

generous handful of fresh coriander/cilantro, finely chopped

1 teaspoon garam masala

½ teaspoon mild, medium or hot chilli powder/ground red chile (depending on taste)

salt and freshly ground black pepper

serves 4 as a side dish or 2 as a main

This Indian lentil dish is packed with flavour and has a soothing, moreish texture that makes it particularly good with "parathas" (Indian flatbreads) or other flatbread.

In a heavy-based shallow saucepan, melt half the butter with half the oil. Add the onion and cook over fairly high heat for about 3 minutes, until it is starting to soften and turn very slightly brown around the edges.

Add the mustard seeds, cover, and wait until you hear them start to pop. Remove the lid and add the fenugreek, ginger and garlic and give everything a good stir for about 30 seconds.

Thoroughly rinse the lentils, then add with the creamed tomatoes and 450 ml/2 cups water to the pan and gently bring to the boil. Simmer, uncovered, for about 15 minutes.

Add the lemon juice and coriander/cilantro and cook for about 5–10 minutes over low heat until the dhal begins to reduce and absorb any excess liquid. The dhal should be almost porridge-like in consistency, ie thick enough that you can scoop it up with a paratha! Season with salt and pepper to taste.

Meanwhile, in a separate pan, heat the remaining butter and oil, add the garam masala and chilli powder/ground red chile and fry for 30 seconds before drizzling all over the dhal.

vietnamese chicken curry

Thanks to the French influence in Vietnamese cuisine, you can enjoy a hearty bowl of chicken curry and then mop up the spiced coconut juices with a crusty baguette – perfect comfort eating!

1 chicken, about 1.8 kg/4 lbs., cut into 10–12 pieces

2 tablespoons mild curry powder

3 tablespoons light olive oil

2 onions, cut into thick wedges

3 garlic cloves, roughly chopped

1 lemongrass stalk, gently bruised

3 dried or fresh bay leaves

2 carrots, each cut into 4 thick chunks

2 x 400-ml/14-oz. cans coconut milk

½ teaspoon sugar

salt and freshly ground black pepper

1–2 baguettes, to serve

serves 4

Put the chicken pieces in a large bowl. Add the curry powder, 1 teaspoon sea salt and some black pepper. Use your hands to toss the chicken until it is evenly coated in the curry mixture.

Put 1 tablespoon of the oil in a casserole dish or large, heavy-based saucepan and set over medium heat. Add half of the chicken pieces and cook for 5 minutes, turning often, until golden brown and crisp. Transfer to a plate. Add another tablespoon of oil to the pan and cook the remaining chicken pieces in the same way. Add them to the first batch. Add the remaining tablespoon of oil to the pan and add the onions, garlic and lemongrass. Cook for 5 minutes, until the onions are golden and soft, stirring occasionally.

Add the bay leaves and carrots to the pan and cook for 2–3 minutes. Increase the heat to high. Add the coconut milk and sugar and bring to the boil, stirring often. Reduce the heat to medium. Cook for 10 minutes. Add all the chicken pieces, except any from the breast, and cook for 10 minutes. The liquid should be gently simmering, not rapidly boiling. Add the remaining chicken and any collected juices and cook for a further 10 minutes, until the chicken is cooked through. Serve with fresh baguette.

big fish stew

500 g/1 lb. small squid, cleaned

8 prawn/shrimp tails (optional)

1 kg/2 lbs. fresh mussels and clams, scrubbed and "beards" removed

1.75 kg/3½ lbs. mixed whole but cleaned fish

flavoured broth

150 ml/⅔ cup extra virgin olive oil

4 leeks, sliced and well washed

4 garlic cloves, finely chopped

300 ml/1¼ cups dry white wine

a large pinch of saffron strands

750 g/1½ lbs. ripe red plum tomatoes, coarsely chopped

2 tablespoons sun-dried tomato paste or purée or 6 sun-dried tomatoes in oil, drained and coarsely chopped

1 teaspoon fennel seeds

1 tablespoon dried oregano

salt and freshly ground black pepper

to serve

lemon wedges

freshly chopped flat leaf parsley

crusty bread

serves 6–8

A deeply flavoured fish broth bursting with the freshest fish and seafood has to be one of the most satisfying bowls of food imaginable. It's also an ideal dish for a group of friends as everyone can tuck in and choose the seafood they prefer.

To make the flavoured broth, heat the olive oil in a large, deep casserole dish and add the leeks and garlic. Cook gently for about 5 minutes until softened. Pour in the white wine and boil rapidly until reduced by half. Add the saffron, tomatoes, tomato paste, fennel seeds and oregano. Pour in 600 ml/2¾ cups water and bring to the boil. Turn down the heat, cover and simmer for 20 minutes until the tomatoes and oil separate.

Start cooking the fish. Add the squid to the pan and poach for 3–4 minutes. Remove with a slotted spoon, put on a plate, cover and keep them warm. Add the prawns/shrimp, if using, and simmer just until opaque. Remove with a slotted spoon and keep warm with the squid. Add the mussels and clams to the broth, cover and boil for a few minutes until they open. Remove with a slotted spoon and keep them warm. Discard any that haven't opened.

Poach all the remaining fish until just cooked, remove from the broth, arrange on a serving dish and set the mussels, squid and prawns/shrimp on top. Taste the broth, which will have all the flavours of the cooked fish in it, and season with salt and pepper if necessary. Moisten the fish with some broth and serve the rest separately with the lemon wedges, chopped parsley and lots of crusty bread.

Enjoying a home-cooked roast lunch is one of life's real pleasures and is often the only leisurely meal in the week that families can enjoy together. Whether your preference is for beef, lamb, pork or chicken, these delicious recipes won't disappoint.

roasts

sweet chilli-glazed ham

4.5-kg/10-lb. ham on the bone

3–4 sprigs of fresh thyme, 2 fresh bay leaves, a sprig of fresh parsley, all firmly tied together in a bundle with kitchen twine

1 carrot, roughly chopped

1 onion, roughly chopped

2 celery sticks, roughly chopped

7–8 black peppercorns

3 whole cloves

330-ml/12-oz. can or bottle of stout beer (eg Guinness or Mackeson)

3 tablespoons sweet chilli/chili sauce

2 tablespoons pure maple syrup

2 tablespoons Dijon mustard

a large casserole dish with a lid

serves 12–14

This is a very simple way of feeding a lot of people, with the sweet chilli glaze making for an irresistibly sticky coating.

Place the ham in the casserole dish, add the herb bundle, carrot, onion, celery, peppercorns, cloves and beer. Top up with cold water until the ham is covered. Set over medium heat and bring to the boil. Reduce the heat, partially cover with the lid and gently simmer for about 3 hours. If it starts to look dry, add only boiling water.

At the end of cooking, remove the dish from the heat and set aside for 20–30 minutes to cool with the ham still in the cooking stock.

Preheat the oven to 200°C (400°F) Gas 6.

Remove the ham from the dish and place on a large board. Cut away and discard the skin, leaving an even layer of fat exposed all over the meat. Place the ham in a large roasting pan and, with a sharp knife, score the fat in a diamond pattern, making sure not to cut through to the meat.

Mix the sweet chilli/chili sauce, maple syrup and mustard thoroughly with a balloon whisk. Spread this glaze evenly over the ham, ensuring it is well coated. Roast the ham in the preheated oven for about 30–40 minutes until nicely browned and the glaze has formed a golden crust. Baste the meat with the glaze that runs into the roasting pan during cooking.

Let the ham rest for a few minutes before carving, then serve hot or cold.

braised pot roast with red wine, rosemary & bay leaves

1.2 kg/3 lbs. braising joint, such as beef brisket, tied

2 tablespoons olive oil

1 onion, halved and thinly sliced

2 celery sticks, thinly sliced

1 large carrot, thinly sliced and cut into half-moons

4 garlic cloves, peeled and sliced

150 g/6 oz. pancetta, very finely chopped

750-ml bottle robust red wine, preferably Italian

400-g/14-oz. can chopped tomatoes

1 fresh or dried bay leaf, 2 large sprigs fresh rosemary, several sprigs fresh parsley, all firmly tied together in a bundle with kitchen twine

3–4 tablespoons capers in brine, drained (optional)

salt and freshly ground black pepper

serves 6

This is the sort of dish that heats the kitchen and fills the house with rich, warming aromas while it cooks. To up the comfort levels, serve with creamy mashed potatoes, soft polenta or macaroni baked in cream with plenty of Parmesan.

Preheat the oven to 180°C (350°F) Gas 4.

Heat the oil in a large casserole dish. Add the beef and cook for about 8–10 minutes, until browned on all sides. Transfer the beef to a plate, season all over with salt and set aside.

Add the onion, celery and carrot to the casserole and cook, stirring often, until browned. Add the garlic and pancetta and cook for 1 minute. Season, then add the wine and tomatoes and bring to the boil. Boil for 1 minute, then add the herb bundle. Return the browned beef to the casserole.

Cover and transfer to the preheated oven. After 1½ hours, remove the casserole dish from the oven and turn the beef over. Pour in some water if the liquid has reduced too much and add the capers, if using. Return to the oven and cook for a further 1½ hours, until the meat is tender.

Serve in slices with the sauce and vegetables spooned over the top and with the accompaniment of your choice.

leg of lamb

1.5-kg/3-lb. leg of lamb

2 tablespoons olive oil

10 juniper berries

3 garlic cloves, crushed

55 g/2 oz. salted anchovies, boned and rinsed, or canned anchovies

1 tablespoon freshly chopped rosemary

2 tablespoons balsamic vinegar

2 sprigs of fresh rosemary

2 fresh bay leaves

300 ml/1¼ cups dry white wine

sprigs of fresh thyme

salt and freshly ground black pepper

a large casserole dish with a lid

serves 6

This Italian-style leg of lamb is braised until cooked and tender, then roasted to colour it. The powerful flavourings melt into the meat, with the anchovies disappearing to leave a lingering salty note.

Preheat the oven to 160°C (325°F) Gas 3.

Trim the lamb of any excess fat. Heat the oil in the casserole dish, add the lamb and brown it all over. Remove the lamb from the dish and cool quickly.

Crush 6 of the juniper berries, the garlic, anchovies and chopped rosemary with a mortar and pestle. Stir in the vinegar and mix to a paste. Using a small, sharp knife, make many small incisions into the lamb. Spread the paste all over the meat, working it into the incisions, then season with salt and pepper.

Put the rosemary sprigs and bay leaves in the casserole dish and set the lamb on top. Pour in the wine. Crush the remaining juniper berries and add to the lamb, then add the thyme. Cover, bring to the boil on top of the stove, then transfer to the preheated oven and braise for 1 hour, turning the lamb every 20 minutes.

Raise the oven temperature to 200°C (400°F) Gas 6. Roast uncovered for another 45 minutes or until browned – the lamb should be very tender and cooked through.

Transfer the lamb to a serving dish and keep it warm. Skim off the fat from the pan, then boil the sauce, adding a little water if necessary and scraping up the sediment. Season with salt and pepper if necessary and serve with the lamb.

roast beef with winter vegetables & garlic crème

This rare roast beef is served with an easy and heavenly garlic crème that you will want to make again and again.

800 g/1¾ lbs. beef rib-eye fillet

1 tablespoon freshly ground black pepper

1 bunch of baby carrots, skin left on and tops trimmed

2 small red onions, cut into thin wedges

1 turnip, cut into quarters

½ small celeriac/celery root, cut into thick batons

1 large parsnip, cut into semi-circles

1 tablespoon light olive oil

garlic crème

1 head of garlic

3 egg yolks

1 teaspoon Dijon mustard

1 teaspoon red wine vinegar

250 ml/1 cup light olive oil

serves 4

Preheat the oven to 180°C (350°F) Gas 4.

To make the garlic crème, wrap the garlic firmly in two layers of foil and cook in the preheated oven for 40 minutes. Remove and let cool. Cut the garlic in half and squeeze the soft flesh directly into the bowl of a food processor. Add the egg yolks, mustard and vinegar and process until smooth. With the motor running, add the oil in a steady stream until it is all incorporated. Transfer to a bowl, cover and refrigerate until needed. Put the beef in a bowl and rub the pepper all over it. Transfer to a plate and refrigerate, uncovered, for at least 3 hours or, ideally, overnight.

When ready to cook the beef, preheat the oven to 220°C (425°F) Gas 7 and put a baking sheet in the oven to heat up.

Put the vegetables onto the preheated baking sheet, drizzle with olive oil and roast for 30 minutes. Turn and roast for a further 10 minutes. Remove from the oven and keep warm.

Heat a frying pan over high heat. When smoking hot, sear the beef fillet for 4 minutes, turning every minute. Put it in a roasting pan and roast in the preheated oven for 10 minutes. Turn the beef and cook for a further 5 minutes. Remove from the oven, cover with foil and let rest for 10 minutes before carving into thick slices to serve.

slow-roasted pork loin with rosemary, madeira & orange

1.5 kg/3 lbs. centre loin of pork

200 ml/¾ cup Madeira wine

100 ml/½ cup freshly squeezed orange juice

2 sprigs of fresh rosemary, bruised

2 oranges, peeled and sliced into 4 slices each

sea salt and freshly ground black pepper

an instant-read thermometer

serves 4

This is a very dense meat, so gentle roasting is the only way to prevent it drying out, giving ample time for the full flavour to develop. Don't forget to spoon out the lovely, orangey juices from the roasting pan – they really complete the dish.

Score the fat with a criss cross pattern and season the meat with plenty of salt and pepper, rubbing it in well. Put a double thickness of kitchen foil in a large roasting pan and turn up the edges. Put in the meat fat side down and pour in the Madeira and juice. Add the rosemary. Leave for about 2 hours if possible.

Preheat the oven to 170°C (325°F) Gas 3.

Put the roasting pan in the middle of the preheated oven and roast for 1 hour.

Carefully turn the meat over, then add the orange slices and about 125 ml/½ cup water if it is starting to dry out. Cook for a further 30 minutes. Then raise the oven temperature to 220°C (425°F) Gas 7 for a final 10 minutes or until an instant-read thermometer registers 80°C (175°F).

Lift the meat out onto a serving dish and arrange the orange slices around. Serve with the cooking juices.

slow-cooked spiced pork belly with apple & fennel

1 tablespoon fennel seeds

2 teaspoons caraway seeds

4 garlic cloves

2 tablespoons olive oil

1 kg/2¼ lbs. pork belly

4 apples, such as Cox's Orange Pippin, cored or not, as preferred

2 fennel bulbs, with feathery tops intact, cut into thick wedges

salt and freshly ground black pepper

serves 4

You can't go far wrong with this slow-cooking method, which produces crispy skin and melt-in-the-mouth meat.

Combine the fennel and caraway seeds, garlic and 1 tablespoon salt in a mortar and pound with a pestle. Stir in 1 tablespoon of the olive oil.

Cut 5-mm/¼-inch deep incisions, spaced 1–2 cm/½ inch apart, across the skin of the pork. Rub the spice mixture into the incisions, and let sit for 1 hour at cool room temperature.

Preheat the oven to 140°C (275°F) Gas 1.

Put the pork in a large roasting pan and cook in the preheated oven for 3 hours in total. (You'll need to remove the pan from the oven 30 minutes before the end of the cooking time to add the apples and fennel.)

Put the remaining oil in a large bowl and season with a little salt and pepper. Add the apples and the fennel bulbs to the bowl and toss until evenly coated in oil. Thirty minutes before the end of the cooking time, remove the pork from the oven and arrange the apples and fennel in the pan. Increase the heat to 220°C (425°F) Gas 7 and return the pan to the oven.

Remove the pork from the oven, cover loosely with foil and let rest for 20 minutes. Serve with the roasted apples and fennel.

roast chicken with herbs & ricotta

250 g/8 oz. ricotta cheese

2 tablespoons finely chopped fresh basil

3 tablespoons finely chopped flat leaf parsley

2 garlic cloves, chopped

2 tablespoons light olive oil

1 teaspoon sea salt

grated zest and freshly squeezed juice of 1 unwaxed lemon

1 chicken, weighing about 1 kg/2½ lbs.

2 lemons, cut in half

kitchen twine

serves 2

There's something about roasting a chicken for a late and leisurely Sunday lunch that makes a fitting end to the weekend. And if you need a new idea for how to roast it, try this – rubbing a herb and ricotta mixture between the skin and meat makes it amazingly succulent.

Preheat the oven to 180°C (350°F) Gas 4.

Put the ricotta in a bowl with the basil, parsley, garlic, 1 tablespoon of the olive oil, sea salt, lemon juice and zest and mix well.

Wash and dry the chicken with kitchen paper/paper towels. Use your hands to carefully separate the skin from the meat, without tearing the skin, and force the ricotta mixture between the skin and the meat. Rub the extra cut lemon halves over the chicken then place them in the cavity of the bird. Tie the legs together with some kitchen twine. Transfer the chicken to a plate, cover with clingfilm/plastic wrap and set aside for 30 minutes.

Put a roasting pan in the preheated oven for 10 minutes to heat up. Pour the remaining olive oil in the roasting pan. Sprinkle sea salt over the chicken, then put the chicken in the pan and roast in the preheated oven for 1 hour.

Remove the chicken from the oven, cover with foil and let cool for 15 minutes before carving.

index

picture credits

Caroline Arber
page 134 ins

Steve Baxter
pages 32, 33, 46, 49, 97, 98

Martin Brigdale
pages 2–6, 50, 53, 55 ins, 56 bg, 61, 66, 67 ins, 69, 71 ins, 85, 86, 88 ins, 89, 90, 93, 94, 109, 111, 112, 124, 126, 127, 131, 136

Peter Cassidy
pages 15 ins, 20 ins, 24, 25, 26, 29, 31, 36 ins, 37, 38, 40, 41, 44 ins, 45, 48, 57, 120, 121, 122 ins, 128, 132, 138

Jonathan Gregson
page 106

Richard Jung
pages 23, 27, 42, 51 ins, 65, 67, 68 ins, 83 ins, 84 ins, 135, 140

Lisa Linder
page 52

William Lingwood
pages 1, 44 bg, 117 ins

Jason Lowe
page 70

Noel Murphy
page 101

Steve Painter
pages 12, 51 bg, 60 ins, 72–75, 76 ins, 77–82, 83 bg, 118, 133

William Reavell
pages 7, 9, 11 ins, 15 bg, 55 bg, 68 bg, 95, 96, 99, 100, 104, 107, 110, 119, 130

Yuki Sugiura
pages 8, 10, 13, 14, 17, 18, 21, 22

Kate Whitaker
pages 11 bg, 16, 19, 20 bg, 28, 35 bg, 36 bg, 39, 43, 54, 58, 59, 60 bg, 62–64, 71 bg, 76 bg, 87, 102, 103, 105, 110, 113–116, 117 bg, 122 bg, 123, 125, 129, 134 bg, 137, 139, 142–144

Isobel Wield
pages 30, 34, 35 ins, 47, 56 ins, 68 bg, 84 bg, 88 bg, 91, 92, 108, 141

recipe credits

Maxine Clark
Bacon, egg & parsley pie
Big fish stew
Cassoulet
Chicken pot pie
Corned beef & sweet potato pasties
Glorious golden fish pie
Lasagne al forno
Leg of lamb
Pasta & cherry tomato pies
Roasted garlic risotto
Triple tomato & basil risotto

Laura Washburn
Apple, parsnip & thyme soup
Asian beef braise with pak-choi
Artichoke, mushroom & olive pasta bake
Baked rigatoni with mozzarella
Braised pot roast with red wine, rosemary & bay leaves
Butternut squash & corn bread pudding
Mashed potato pie with bacon, leeks & cheese
Moussaka
Pepper beef quesadilla
Root vegetable gratin

Tonia George
Dukkah & harissa sausage rolls
Harrira
Lamb & bean tagine with buttered couscous
Minestrone soup
Parsnip, chorizo & chestnut soup
Roast chicken, garlic & watercress soup
Smoked haddock & bean soup
Split pea & sausage soup
Vietnamese beef pho

Dan May
Cajun-spiced, soufléd baked potatoes
Creole seafood burritos
Huevos rancheros
Patatas bravas
puttanesca pasta sauce
Spicy vegetable chowder
Sweet chilli-glazed ham
Tarka dhal

Annie Rigg
Baked large pasta shells
Creamy pancetta & onion tart
Sole goujons
Spiced fried chicken
Sticky spare ribs

Ross Dobson
Roast beef with winter vegetables & garlic crème
Roast chicken with herbs & ricotta
Slow-cooked spiced pork belly with apple & fennel
Thai-style golden seafood noodle salad
Vietnamese chicken curry

Jordan Bourke
Aubergine and tomato gratin
Bibimbap
Polenta pizza
Wild mushroom & leek risotto

Jennifer Joyce
A bowl of red
Corned beef hash
Wicked mac & Cheese

Nadia Arumugam
Beef chow mein
Sticky orange beef lettuce wraps

Sunil Vijayakar
Lamb biryani
Lamb rogan josh

Brian Glover
Roasted squash, chickpea & chorizo soup

Sonia Stevenson
Slow-roasted pork loin with rosemary, madeira & orange